CONTENTS

DEDICATION

For Grandmama Graves and Grandma Fledderjohann: I'm glad to be your granddaughter and I love you; and in loving memory of Grandpa F. and Poppa.

—J.E.L.

For Grandma and Grandpa Boynton with love; and in joyful memory of Nana, Boppa, and Grandma-in-Heaven.

—K.B.T.

ACKNOWLEDGMENTS

Thank you to all the amazing and generous consultants—both grandparents and grandchildren—who shared their hopes, ideas, and memories with us.

Grand Days Consultants

Carolyn Beachy
Dr. Richard/Mrs. Hazel Bimler
Rev. Robert P./Jeanne B. Blahnik
Fred W. Cowan
Boyd E. and Karen S. Davis
Eileen Fledderjohann
Elizabeth G. Fledderjohann
Matthew Fledderjohann
James and Ann Hickey
Margaret Rickers Hinchey

Sharon L. Kelly
Charles S. Mueller, Sr.
Margaret Pinney
Steve and Kay Russell
Walter M. and Leota H. Schoedel
Ted Schroeder
Jane Smith
Ben and Liebe Stutzman
Grace Wiley
Maddie Wiley

Special thanks to the "Think Tank" group brought together by the Association of Lutheran Older Adults. It was your heart for helping grandparents pass on their legacies to their grandchildren that inspired this book.

INTRODUCTION

What are your hopes for your grandchildren? To be "successful" (whatever that means)? To be wealthy and popular? To own a vacation home or a yacht? To teach or coach at a Big Ten school? Probably not. Real grandparents contributed to this book, and none of them mentioned these sorts of goals for their grandchildren.

One said, "I hope when they're older they will want to be with me and love me. Maybe they'll even say to their friends, 'I learned this or that from my grandma!' I hope they don't forget me!" (Grandmom Hazel)

Granddad Rich added, "I pray frequently that I will live long enough to see them all find life partners who also love the Lord. How wonderful if I could have the blessings of great-grandchildren to know and love!"

Pops Bob and Grams Jeanne said, "We want each of our grandchildren to embrace who God created them to be—which means *knowing* who they are (and who they aren't), *liking* who they are, and *being* who they are in God."

Other grandparents expressed similar desires—for their grandchildren to love and serve God. How can *you* be involved in your grandchild's spiritual journey? By being involved in her life. By talking to him about things that matter—and most things matter somehow, but you have to discern *how* they matter.

In this book you'll find all sorts of ideas for ways you can spend time with your grandchild—from simple, traditional ideas such as fishing or baking a cake, to modern technological pastimes like playing Wii and text-messaging. Every single suggestion probably won't be up your alley, but some will be, and others can easily be adapted to fit your geographic location, interests, and resources. We've tried to include all types.

But before you dive in, remember: The time you spend with your grandchildren will be what they remember most about you. They will probably not know much about what you did at work or the sorts of grades you received at school. They won't care that much about your clubs or organizations—much less understand them. But they will be formed, shaped, and molded by being with you and getting to know you as you are.

So spend lots of time with your grandchildren. Do fun things! Do what they want, but introduce them to the variety of joys in which we can participate on this earth. And, most of all, love them. Give them hugs. Say, "I love you. I care about you." And let your actions follow suit.

TIPS FOR USING THIS BOOK

We've created this book to both include fun ideas—and to help you grow your relationship with your grandchildren. Here are a few things you'll want to be looking for as you use *Grand Days*.

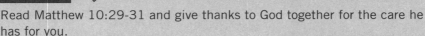 BRIDGE BUILDERS

Whenever you see this, you'll find suggestions for conversations you can have with your grandchildren to get to know them better and deepen your relationship with them.

Pass It On features are suggestions for questions or conversation starters that you can use to pass on your faith or discuss spiritual matters.

> **PASS IT ON**
>
> Read Matthew 10:29-31 and give thanks to God together for the care he has for you.

Live far away from your grandkids? **Stay Connected** insights and ideas are perfect for growing closer even if miles separate you.

STAY CONNECTED

If your grandchild lives far away, purchase a bird-watching book for his region of the country. When you visit, go on a walk together in a nature preserve or park and try to identify some of the birds. Or, if you've made a birdhouse for your house, take photographs of the birdhouse or feeder and send them by e-mail to your grandchild!

(example)

How do you want your grandchildren to remember you?

All sorts of grandparents and a few grandchildren shared ideas and insights for this book and many of them included memories of their own grandparents. Some of these are spread throughout the chapters, but each of the memories depict real, imperfect people who left a strong imprint on their grandchild's memory.

- "Whenever we would drive into Grandmama and Papa's narrow gravel driveway, I would see them come out of the screen door to greet us. Grandmama would often wait on the porch while Papa would meet us at our van. Their home always had the same musty cold smell and the candy jar was usually full."

  –Liebe, granddaughter

- "My grandpa was a very organized man who always had his ducks in a row—which was a bit unlike my own laid-back father. So, whenever Grandpa would visit us, he would organize the tools in our shed. As I grew older, I felt a bit embarrassed before Grandpa would come because I knew he would feel the need to organize our tools."

  —Ben, grandson

- "I have interestingly frightening memories of the one grandfather I knew—Pop. He smoked cigarettes and blew the smoke into our faces when we were too near, and then he'd drop ashes onto Mama Smith's (my grandmother's) clean floors. He wore false teeth for as long as I knew him, and he would loosen them with his tongue and rattle them in his mouth when he'd look at us. He was gruff and growly, but he loved Mama Smith. She could, by mere suggestion, get him to do whatever she had in mind."

  —Elizabeth, granddaughter

- "My grandparents were always 'old'! I want to be more active and responsive to my grandkids than they were with me."

  —Grandad Rich

- "We had good role models for grandparenting. Our grandparents were always considered part of the family and were involved in the life of the family without ever being overbearing. We would like to follow in their footsteps."

  —Grandpa Jim and Grandma Ann

Let's Make Something

Projects to Do With Your Grandchild

Do you remember the first thing you ever made? Was it a macaroni necklace? a mud pie? a big mess? Was there anyone to encourage you in your work and play as you developed your fine motor skills?

Making things can be a wonderful pastime. A large part of our Christian narrative includes the understanding that God made things. He made the world: daffodils, llamas, gravity, stars, people. And he took great joy in his creation because he pronounced it "good."

Whether you have four thumbs or you're a master craftsman, you'll find fun ideas of things you can teach to or explore with your grandchild in this chapter. Use the time spent together making things to set an example of how work can be fulfilling and what it means for our work— no matter what we do—to glorify God.

I'd like my grandchildren to learn how to be hard workers and to find pleasure in their efforts.

—Grandma Jane, grandmother of 11

Let's Build a Birdhouse

Whether you or your grandchild lives in the city, suburbs, or country, you can make a birdhouse. If you (or the child's parents) don't have a yard, consider giving the birdhouse to a friend or a church. You can find simple kits for birdhouses at many craft and hobby stores, and there are plenty of traditional wooden birdhouse instructions on the Internet. Even if you don't own a single tool or have a workbench, you can make a birdhouse out of simple, recycled, around-the-house materials.

Making a wooden birdhouse with your grandchild will probably take longer than a day, so you can spread this activity out for the course of a longer visit or subsequent return visits.

☞ CHECK IT OUT

Birdhouses and feeders don't just have to be made out of wood. Here are websites that use alternate materials to build birdhouses:

- Coffee can birdhouse at www.allfreecrafts.com/nature/bee-birdhouse.shtml

- Gourd or milk/juice carton birdhouses at www.thekidsgarden.co.uk/BuildABirdHouse.html

- Milk carton birdhouses at www.easy-child-crafts.com/easy-kid-craft-idea.html

PROFILE

Grandparents of 11 grandchildren, Leonard and Carolyn Beachy strive to get to know each of them individually and zero in on their interests and passions. "We try to provide both opportunities and materials for them to develop their interests," says Carolyn. "If one loves music, we're privileged to join with their parents in giving a gift of drums and a guitar; a grandchild who loves art will receive paints, brushes, easels, and so on." Seeking to help them develop their strengths and interests brings the Beachys great joy. "I'm their cheerleader—and so is their grandpa," Carolyn remarks.

Once your birdhouse is made, pay attention to the birds in your yard. Consider purchasing a bird-watching guide and sharing it with your grandchild. Does making a home for the birds show your care for them? Why do we care for things God has made? Discuss how God cares for birds and human beings. Read Matthew 10:29-31 and give thanks to God together for the care he has for you.

Get Creative with Your Birdhouse!

When decorating your birdhouse, be as creative as you can! Here are fun ideas to get you started:

- Build or paint your birdhouse to look like your grandchild's or your house or church.

- Glue twigs on the outside of the birdhouse to make it look like a log cabin.

- Paint the outside of the birdhouse to look like a cat—with the opening or door the cat's mouth!

- Camouflage the birdhouse so it blends in with the yard or tree.

 STAY CONNECTED

If your grandchild lives far away, purchase a bird-watching book for his region of the country. When you visit, go on a walk together in a nature preserve or park and try to identify some of the birds. Or, if you've made a birdhouse for your house, take photographs of the birdhouse or feeder and send them by e-mail to your grandchild!

We have a bird feeder and it has been fun teaching my young granddaughter Eliana the different names of all the birds . . . she has a very good memory!

—Grandma Ann, grandmother of two

My Grandpa Mueller let me build a wagon bed when I was 10 with a lot of support and little correction—bad as the end product was. It made my day!

—Grandpa Charles, grandfather of 17

Growing Step by Step

Enrich your backyard with fun memories—and mark your grandchildren's growth—by making handprint-themed garden steppingstones together. In most craft stores, kits with all the needed supplies to make basic cement garden steppingstones are readily available; they range in price from about $10 to $15. You can also buy embellishments such as colored, round stones, cut glass (to create a mosaic effect), and letters to "stamp" into the wet cement to create words.

With your grandchild, draw a plan for your stone before you start because once you've poured the wet cement, you'll need to work fast! Be sure to include a handprint of your grandchild in the design; over time, you can create additional stones together and watch the handprints grow bigger and bigger.

 BRIDGE BUILDER

This is a natural opportunity to talk with your grandchild about growing up. Ask her questions like:

- What do you want to be when you grow up? Why?

- If you could live anywhere in the world when you grow up, where would you want to live? Why?

- Who are some people that you want to be like when you grow up?

When my 2-year-old daughter was picking my mother's flowers, my husband and I went outside to stop her from picking any of the blossoms. Mother put things into perspective when she said, "Let her pick them and enjoy them now. If she were to die, people would send flowers and she would never be able to enjoy them. This is the time for her to pick them if she wants to."

—Elizabeth, mother and granddaughter

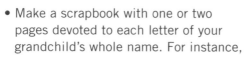

Let's Make a Scrapbook

Scrapbooking is a very popular hobby these days, and people of all ages can participate. Make a scrapbook with your grandchild. You can make traditional chronological scrapbooks, or you can use one of the following thematic ideas:

- Make a scrapbook with one or two pages devoted to each letter of your grandchild's whole name. For instance, "Ellen" would include "Excited About Presidents" (showing pictures of Ellen at different presidential museums), "Loves Learning" (containing a report card and some photos from school), "Lettuce Garden" (presenting photos of Ellen, her garden, and a salad), "Evergreen Terrace" (telling her street name, with photos of neighbors), and "Nodding Off" (showing a photo of Ellen sleeping).

- Make a book to honor a family member who has died. Use photos from that person's life, and write out memories. The grandchild can keep this book to help remember the past. This would be a great artifact to take to family reunions.

- Make a family history album. Include information about your grandparents, family trees, old photographs, and stories from several generations. (Contact other relatives and ask them to contribute stories and photographs.)

🌉 BRIDGE BUILDER

While you're making a scrapbook with your grandchild, discuss how your growing-up experiences are similar and different. In addition to listening to your grandchild's answers, be sure you share your answers. Here are some questions to get the conversation rolling:

- When have you felt like you didn't fit in?

- What is the best part about growing up? the worst part?

- What did/do you fear about being an adult?

- If you could be any age, which age would you choose? Why?

- Do you wish any relationships with your family members were different? Why? What would this look like?

Make Music

Music is a wonderful gift to share with others. Here are ideas for ways you and your grandchild (musical or not!) can participate in music together:

For those who can sing or play an instrument:

- If you and your grandchild can both play musical instruments, learn to play duets together. It's easy to find pieces with piano accompaniment for most instruments, and there are plenty of simple piano duet books available. This would make a great gift!

- Sing songs together. There are many songs from camp, Sunday school, and church you knew in your childhood that your grandchild doesn't know. Teach these to him.

- Focus on sacred music together, such as hymns. Choose a "theme song" that you can always sing or play together. Discuss what the song means to you. A great online hymn resource is www.cyberhymnal.org. You can read the texts and hear the melodies of over 6,900 hymns!

PROFILE

Special Needs, Special Moments

Right after she was born, my granddaughter Lily was transported to Children's Mercy Hospital for possible heart surgery after the pediatrician confirmed she had Down syndrome. Her surgery was postponed, but over the next two weeks many tests were done and many doctors entered her life.

After a few days, her dad needed to return to work, so her mother (my daughter) and I spent each day in the neonatal intensive care unit with Lily. She is a beautiful little girl—full of energy; she kicked and kicked.

When I was alone by Lily's bedside, I would sing "Jesus Loves You" over and over again. Music is not my strong point and typically I only stay on key when I hear someone else singing, but during those days my voice sounded like a clear, perfect pitch. It was as if God was telling me how much he loved Lily—and all of us—and reassuring me that he would be with us in the days ahead.

—Grams Kay

15

👉 CHECK IT OUT

For fun music to sing with your youngest grandchildren, check out *Whirl-n-Worship*. School-aged kids will have a great time singing along with you as you listen to *Shine! Greatest Hits* together. These are available at www.group.com.

For those who can play the radio:

• Listen to your grandchild's music. As different as it may sound to you, try not to act appalled by the band name or style of music. Ask your grandchild why she likes this music, what it means to her, and what it tells her about the world. If you are curious about the lyrics, most song words can be found on the Internet.

• Go to a classical concert together. Before you go, find a recording of the music that will be played (look at your local library or on www.iTunes.com) and listen to it together to become familiar with the music. Talk about the sounds. How does this music make you feel? What do you imagine when you hear it?

> **PASS IT ON**
>
> There are a lot of songs based on Scripture texts. Make a collection of either recorded or printed music based on Scripture songs. Sing these songs with your grandchild. The use of music is an excellent way to memorize Scripture.

🕊 BRIDGE BUILDER

If you listen to your grandchild's music, tell him about the type of music you listened to when you were his age. Did your parents approve? How did the music make you feel? If possible, share some of this music with your grandchild and compare it to the popular music of today.

When I married, I was really able to get to know my grandmother-in-law. After work I would stop by her house and visit. It was a hard time for her because Grandpa's dementia was getting worse. Sometimes we would sew together. Sometimes we'd just chat. She showed me how to quilt and told me the names of some of the special stitches.

—Liebe, granddaughter

Let's Sew!

If you have a sewing machine and know how to sew, you can teach your grandchild a useful lifelong skill. Take your grandchild to the fabric store and allow him or her to select material and a pattern for a simple project. Here are a few projects that you can find easy patterns for:

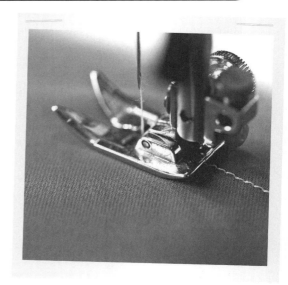

- skirt
- pajama bottoms
- pillow
- poncho
- vest

PROFILE

For gifts, Grandma Jane makes many of her grandchildren's presents or she takes them on little trips because she's noticed that most children these days already have enough possessions.

"A memory is better to give them," she says, and adds that making gifts "can be harder and not always cheaper, but it shows your love and that you were thinking about them." One year, she made pajamas for two of her grandchildren. She included hoods that could attach to the PJs so the children could dress up to be a dog or a rabbit. They were a big hit! "The hoods lasted a lot longer than the pajamas," she says.

When my oldest granddaughter (about 12 years old at the time) was visiting, she wanted to sew a pair of yellow pants. It was a lot of work for her, but we got it done. She is still interested in sewing for herself and she loves fabrics!

—Grandma Jane, grandmother of 11

Knit or Crochet

Can you knit or crochet? Many children learn to knit or crochet from their grandmothers, and this is a craft best learned by doing it with someone else rather than just reading a book. Help your grandchild make a simple project: a doll afghan, a washcloth, or a scarf for a first project. For younger children, use large-sized needles or hooks.

Be Fashion Designers!

Get two plain white T-shirts—one your size and one your grandchild's size. Then use fabric paints (or fabric markers) for each design and decorate a T-shirt for the other person. When the paint has dried, put on the T-shirts and wear them on an outing together. If you both agree, choose a theme to help you design your shirts—a matching color scheme, for example, or pictures of a butterfly you saw.

Crafts to Learn Together

- Candle making
- Tatting
- Soap making
- Quilling
- Beading or jewelry making
- Quilting
- Woodworking
- Metalworking
- Drawing
- Painting
- Sculpture
- Pottery
- Model making
- Sewing

PROFILE

Fun—Not Perfection

As a young boy, Ted remembers doing several projects with his grandfather; though the time together was special, what sticks in his mind is his grandfather's drive for perfection. His insistence that projects be done just right often emptied them of their fun.

"I resolved to be a different kind of grandparent," says Ted. "I like to do projects with my grandkids. We don't worry too much about a stray mark here, a slightly crooked line there, or something that does not exactly match. But we have a good time at it! And in the end, the project doesn't look half bad. Once my grandson Justin and I made a model. The glue got a little liberal and the decals weren't quite straight, but he thought it was great—and I did, too."

Junk Sculpture

Gather up a variety of odds and ends—bottle caps, buttons, chenille wires, wire, paint, bits of wood, scraps of fabric—pretty much anything. You can either make a sculpture with your grandchild or each of you make your own. Give your grandchild a theme to work with, such as "Create an imaginary animal (or silly hat or Christmas tree ornament) with these supplies" and see what she comes up with. Make sure to provide workable adhesive so that the sculpture—large or small—will stay together.

PASS IT ON

Discuss the word *redeemed*. What does it mean to redeem and be redeemed? How can our junk sculpture redeem things we had previously thought of as trash?

10 Project Supplies to Have on Hand for Instant Fun!

1. Construction paper
2. Kid-friendly safety scissors
3. Crayola Model Magic
4. Glitter glue pens
5. Four varieties of glue: white liquid glue, glue stick, tacky glue (for fabric), Mod Podge (for decoupage)
6. A stack of old magazines
7. Colorful yarn
8. Tongue depressors or craft sticks
9. Sculpey clay
10. Pieces of felt

Sitting with me in the back of our station wagon, Papa once taught me how to draw a bird in flight. His technique was just a slight variation on the standard "∨" silhouette, but there was a finesse about his work that made these birds something special.

—Matthew, grandson

Learn to Dance

Many community centers offer adult education courses, including dance classes. Usually these classes are for ages 15 and up. Consider taking a dance or movement class with your older grandchild. Tap and square dancing are fun intergenerational dances, or, for the more daring, try ballet.

 BRIDGE BUILDER

What sort of dances were popular when you were growing up? Were you even allowed to dance? Share stories with your grandchild and show him how you used to dance when you were his age. Ask him to show you how he likes to dance now.

TIP

Afraid your grandchild will be embarrassed by taking a class with her grandma? Ask her to make sure, or pair up with another grandma and granddaughter so you won't be the only intergenerational duet in the class!

Embrace Technology!

WDYT your grandchild is typing on that phone while FOFL?

Stupified by text lingo? (Those abbreviations mean "What do you think?" and "Falling on floor laughing.") Remember when there were just one or two video games that were confusing enough to understand? Ask your grandchild to help you understand this new world.

Primarily, make sure you have your grandchild's e-mail address. E-mail or IM (send an instant message to) your grandchild often. Don't have an instant messenging program? Ask your grandchild to help you set one up. They're free to download.

If your grandchild is interested, join a networking site like Facebook as a great way to connect with her on a daily basis. The site is free to join and fun—you can communicate with all your grandchildren and your own friends from long ago! Ask your grandchild to help you set up a personal page, or you can figure it out on your own and surprise him!

To save money on long-distance charges if you aren't near your grandchildren, consider using Skype. Skype is a program that can be downloaded onto your computer and your grandchildren's computer; it enables Skype users to talk to each other for *free*. You can also stay in touch over the miles by each using a webcam—this way, you can actually *see* each other when you talk online.

STAY CONNECTED

If your grandchild lives far away from you, using technology is one of the best ways to keep in touch with her. Consider dropping her a note via e-mail or even text message several times a week just to see how she's doing.

Let's Have a Garage Sale!

In the spring, summer, or fall, help each other go through your closets, drawers, and cabinets (both at your house and your grandchild's room—or his house, if it's OK with his parents). Set aside all the items you no longer use that are in good condition for a garage sale. When you have enough items, organize them by type and plan a garage sale. Be sure your grandchild is included in every step of the planning, as well as in the actual sale event.

A week before the event, take out an advertisement in the paper including your address and the types of items that will be for sale (examples: baby clothing, double bed, kitchen table, CDs) and the time of the sale. If you don't want people arriving early, specify "No early birds!" You can also make posters together to advertise in your neighborhood.

Make sure you have at least $50 in change—including $5 and $1 bills and coins. Put the money in a cash box, and make sure the cash box is always attended by someone. Helping a younger grandchild with this task is a great way to teach about making change (and can help with math skills). Older kids can usually handle this without your supervision.

Be willing to change prices for items if your primary goal is to sell them. If not, don't be insulted when people offer surprisingly low amounts for nice things.

Discuss with your grandchild the possibility of all proceeds from the garage sale being donated to a local charity. If you decide to do this, make sure there are posters visible at the garage sale noting that "All proceeds will be donated to Second Harvest" (or whichever neighborhood association or charity you choose)—it may encourage people to pay a little more!

Spa in a Jar

A nice, long soak in the tub is sometimes just what the doctor ordered after a long day of work—or after a long night of homework for your teenage granddaughter! So make some scented bath salts together as a way to pamper yourselves.

Simply mix the following together in a large plastic or glass bowl:

- 2 cups Epsom salt

- 2 teaspoons baking soda

Next, add 10 to 15 drops of an essential oil while continuing to stir the salt mix. Some great scents to consider are rose, lavender, rosemary, vanilla, peppermint, or eucalyptus.

Pour the prepared mix into a glass jar with a lid. To use, simply add about ¼ cup as you draw a bath.

PASS IT ON

A Show of Love

Help your young grandchildren show love to their parents by leading them in making some spontaneous "I love you!" cards for their mom and dad. Make a few sample cards before they arrive to give them ideas, and have a table of supplies ready to go. Then, when you're ready to do the project together, say something like "Your mommy and daddy love you *so* much. Did you know that? It would mean so much to them if we could surprise them with a special message about how much *we* love *them*."

Work together with your grandchildren, complimenting them on their card designs. As you work, you may want to talk about how God gave their parents a very special job: raising them! Encourage them to obey their parents (Ephesians 6:1-3). You may also want to share with them that God is like a parent to us—God loves us like a parent does (and much more!), and we are to obey and love God in return.

PROFILE

It was a cold, dreary winter day in Indianapolis—about the furthest thing from a warm, sunny day at the beach that you could imagine! My kids and their visiting cousin were sick of being housebound, but "Ammy" was here to visit and she was determined to brighten up the scene! So she led the three cousins, ages 1 to 4, in a fun project she called "Ocean in a Bottle."

Each child had a clear, recyclable bottle (with a lid), and bit by bit, Ammy helped the kids add the following ingredients (all purchased for less than $10):

- very fine sand
- a few small shells
- a few "starfish" (metallic star-shaped sequins)
- a few ocean creatures (cut out of foamlike craft paper)
- some "seaweed" (snips off a plastic aquarium plant)
- a few shakes of clear and colored glitter

Then Ammy helped the kids use a funnel to fill the "ocean" with water. The caps were replaced and sealed on tightly with a glue gun, and then the hurricanes of young kids shaking and swirling their oceans began! The bottles brought delight for days on end...and were a nice imaginative break from the snow outside!

Winning Together

Games and Other Wacky Ways to Have Fun

They were my first late nights, lasting well into the night (past 8 p.m.!). They were raucous parties filled with laughter, serious snacking on snickerdoodle cookies, and some cutthroat competition...against Grandma!

It was a staple part of every visit to Grandma and Grandpa's house for my family: late nights around the kitchen table learning and playing card games until we kids were too tired to stay awake any longer. When we were little, I suspect Grandpa and Grandma let us win a lot because now, as adults, my siblings and I have discovered that they are *awfully* tough to beat (especially Grandma!).

Games—from the most simple scribble of Tic-Tac-Toe to an elaborate Monopoly tournament—are great family "glue." As you laugh, conspire, and celebrate each other's victories, your relationships are cemented. You form bonds of love and joy and memory that will help you stick closer and closer together over the years.

In this chapter you'll find all sorts of games: active and passive, indoor and outdoor, old-fashioned and brand-new, high-tech and no-tech. Pick the ideas that suit you best, and plan for some fun family glue time with your grandkids.

By the way, be sure to let them win!

If there is a word that describes grandparenting most closely, it is encourager.

—Grandpa Ted, grandfather of five

Bumper Bowling

At most bowling alleys, a large "bumper" can be placed into each gutter, preventing any gutter balls and greatly increasing the chance that at least one pin will be knocked down in each attempt. Even preschool-aged kids can bumper-bowl with a little help. You'll have lots of fun laughing together and cheering for each other!

Some bowling alleys have special times set aside for children's bowling, bumper bowling, or even "glow bowling," in which the regular lights in the bowling alley are replaced by ultraviolet lights, causing the pins, the balls, and everyone's clothing and teeth to glow!

Kick the Can

Do you have memories of playing Kick the Can in your neighborhood as a child? It's a game that kids have loved for generations, though most children today probably don't know what it is. Next time your grandkids come over, teach them how to play—they're sure to love it!

Supplies: empty tin can, chalk

Number of players: 3 or more

Setup: Draw a circle (5 to 8 feet in diameter) on the pavement and put the tin can in the middle.

How to play: Select one player to be "It," who stands inside the circle while everyone else stands outside the circle. His goal is to guard the tin can; the other players are aiming to run into the circle and kick the can as far outside the circle as they can.

When the can is kicked, all the players (except for "It") run away and try to quickly hide where he can't see them. At the same time, he runs to get the can and bring it back inside the circle.

When he has brought the can back, he yells out "Freeze!" or "Stop!" At this

 TIP

3 Things to Do With Tin Cans
- play Kick the Can
- make tin-can stilts
- make a tin-can telephone

PROFILE

Granddad Rich likes to play a game he invented and named "Getz" with his grandchildren. Here's how he describes it: "Lie down on the floor and try to grab the grandkids as they run and jump on you—ouch!"

point, everyone has to halt right where they are. If he can see anyone out in the open (who didn't get to a hiding place fast enough), he calls out the person's name and that player must now sit right outside the circle as his prisoner.

Next, he seeks to find and capture the other prisoners—they are captured as soon as he sees them and says their names. (A more active variation is to have him actually catch or tag the other players in order to imprison them.) Here's the catch: When he leaves the circle to find other prisoners, any of the other players can sneak out of hiding and try to run back to the circle and kick the can out again. If that happens, all the prisoners are freed and the game starts over.

Whoever is the last player to be caught or imprisoned becomes "It" during the next round.

Pass the Time

Kids can get bored easily, especially if they're stuck in the backseat on a long car ride, are tagging along on a shopping trip, or are in a waiting room for an appointment. Transform dull times into fun interactions with these easy games that don't require any supplies.

Rock, Paper, Scissors
Number of players: 2
How to play: Use hand signals to face off in this simple competition. Each player makes a fist and both count to 3 together. On "3," both players each quickly make one of the following symbols with their hand: Rock (closed fist), Paper (open palm, face down), or Scissors (two fingers in a V shape, like scissors).

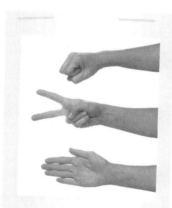

- Rock beats Scissors (because a rock can smash scissors)
- Scissors beats Paper (because scissors can cut paper)
- Paper beats Rock (because paper can cover a rock)

Alphabet Shopping
Number of players: 2 or more
How to play: The first player says, "I went to the store and bought an..." and then adds a word that begins with the letter "a" such as *apple, avocado*, or even *alligator*. The next player repeats the phrase including the "a" word and then adds a "b" word such as *blueberry* or *burger*. Players continue taking turns adding items in alphabetical order, each time trying to remember and repeat the entire shopping list beginning with "a."

You may not live close enough to your grandchild to play games, but you can have lots of fun playing Tic-Tac-Toe by mail! Send your grandchild a fun card with a Tic-Tac-Toe game drawn inside; be the first to place an X or an O. Invite your grandchild to make the next move and mail it back to you (be sure to include a self-addressed stamped envelope to make the process simple). Keep the game going through the mail until someone wins (preferably your grandchild!), and add fun notes or words of encouragement each time you send the game back.

Add On

Number of players: 2 or more

How to play: The first player says a two-word phrase or two-word description such as "chocolate milk" or "sunny day" or "planet Earth." The next player then takes the last word of the phrase and makes it the first word of a new two-word (or three-word) phrase (or a word that can act as a two- or three-word phrase). This pattern is repeated until players are unable to come up with more ideas. Players should try to work together to think of words and phrases that will be helpful to the other players. Also, you can bend the rules a little by adding or dropping suffixes as needed or intermixing words with similar sounds. Here are a few examples:

- Example: good night; night light; light as air; air ball; ball game; game night

- Example (with rule bending): finger paint; painted turtle; turtle soup; super man; manatee; T-shirt

We have a lot of property and not a very good yard, so one weekend Grandpa buried $10 worth of quarters all over the yard and let the kids use his metal detector to find them. The kids found a few quarters and other metal things. They had a great time, and their dad couldn't believe the mess we let them make. When the kids think of it again, we will have another exploration party.

—Grandma Jane

🛠️ BRIDGE BUILDER

Apples to Apples (or Apples to Apples Junior) is a fun family game that can help you get to know your grandchildren better. In this card game from Mattel, family members group cards together based on their own opinions or word associations. There's never any "right" answer—in each round, one player is the "judge," who selects the winning word based on his own whims. As you play together, you'll discover who among you is always a joker, who's serious and literal, and who is just plain unpredictable!

Great Games

Scout out garage sales, clearance racks, and discount stores to fill a closet shelf with a few favorite children's games you can play with your grandkids when they visit. Here are some great standbys that are frequently rated as top games by children's magazines:

Pre-K and Elementary
- Candy Land
- Chutes and Ladders
- Cootie
- Hungry Hungry Hippos
- Memory
- Mouse Trap
- Operation

Older Elementary
- Battleship
- Boggle
- Clue
- Connect Four
- Life
- Trivial Pursuit Junior Edition

🛠️ BRIDGE BUILDER

Playing games can help you teach your grandchild about being a good winner and a good loser, and about playing as a team. As you play games together, share stories from your own life about a time you might have been a sore loser and how God helped you learn to be more gracious. Or demonstrate encouraging words and help your grandchildren learn to build each other up through games instead of making others feel bad by placing blame.

⬤▬ STAY CONNECTED ⬤

Buy a fun children's puzzle that matches your grandchild's ability level—also be sure to pick up four large manila envelopes. Mix up the puzzle pieces and divide them evenly into the four envelopes. Cut out or photocopy the picture on the front of the puzzle, and put it in the first envelope. Send your grandchild one envelope each week for a month (stick a letter inside, too). He will have a great time assembling the puzzle "with" you!

Classic Games

Introduce your grandkids to the pleasure of some simple, "quiet," classic games your own grandparents might have played during their childhood such as Marbles, Dominoes, or Jacks.

Ring Taw (Marbles)

Supplies: chalk or string; 6 or more small marbles; 2 or more large marbles
Number of players: 2 or more
Setup: Use chalk (or a long string) to create a circle on the ground (about 3 or 4 feet in diameter). Create a smaller circle (about 1 foot in diameter or smaller) inside the larger one. Place all the small marbles inside the inner circle.
How to play: Popular since the time of the early American settlers, Ring Taw will still delight kids today! Each player gets one large marble called a Shooter; the small marbles within the inner circle are called Nibs. All players stand or kneel outside the large circle. One at a time, they "shoot" (or roll) their Shooter toward the Nibs; their goal is to knock the Nibs out of the inner circle. If any Nibs are knocked out of the inner circle, that player gets to keep them. Players continue to take turns shooting at the Nibs until they've all been knocked out of the inner circle. Whoever has the most Nibs wins the game.

Draw (Dominoes)

Supplies: dominoes set
Number of players: 2 or more
Setup: Place all dominoes face down on a table.
How to play: A game of Dominoes (dominoes are also called "bones") is not only fun to play, but it's a great way to help young grandchildren learn skills like counting and matching. Play begins when players takes turns drawing dominoes until each has three. The remaining dominoes are left facedown; these leftovers are called the "bone yard."

Any player who has a doublet (a domino with matching sides) lays it down first. (If no one has a doublet, find one in the bone yard to start the game.) The next player then places a domino (against the doublet) that has a matching number of dots on one side. Players continue taking turns creating a chain (or "train") of dominoes by placing dominoes next to each other as they match the number of dots.

Whenever a player does *not* have a domino that matches, he needs to draw dominoes from the bone yard until a matching one is drawn.

The game ends when a player is able to lay down all of his dominoes.

Jacks

Supplies: 6 to 10 metal jacks; 1 small rubber bouncy ball

Number of players: 2 or more

Setup: Set jacks on a smooth, hard surface (such as a cement sidewalk or a kitchen floor)

How to play: There are several variations of this game—you can select one that best fits your grandchild's ability level. The basic idea of the game is that a player sits or kneels on the floor and then throws down the ball so that it bounces once high in the air; she then quickly attempts a task with the jacks before the ball hits the ground (the player should attempt to catch the ball).

One simple way to play is using numbers. Right as the player is about to bounce the ball, another player shouts out a number (1 through 10). The first player then attempts to quickly scoop up that exact number of jacks before catching the ball.

The other fun way to play is to take turns doing various tricks while the ball is in the air. In one trick, called "Horses in a Stable," a player makes a "stable" by putting all four fingertips of one hand on the ground. One at a time, the player uses the other hand to usher the "horses" (jacks) into the doors of the stable (the V openings between the fingers). The player stables one horse with each bounce. (You could have fun making up your own silly or challenging jacks tricks with your grandchild!)

Fishing Trip on the Couch

Your young grandchild (1-year-old through pre-K) will love playing this game with you! First, draw, color, and cut out 10 or more fish on pieces of paper; affix a metal paper clip to the mouth of each fish. Next, create a fishing pole by attaching a string to the end of a pole and then tying a strong magnet to the end of the string. Set up a fishing area by laying a blue blanket (the water) behind a couch; spread the fish out on the blanket. And if you have several grandchildren, older siblings can be involved in helping to create the fishing game for their little sister or brother.

When your grandchild arrives, invite her to go on a fishing trip with you. Imagine together that you are getting ready for the trip, and then climb into your "boat" (the couch). Teach your grandchild how to catch the fish by dragging the magnet across the water toward the mouths of the fish and then reeling 'em in. Celebrate each catch!

TIP

Old-Fashioned Games
- Rock School
- Red Rover
- Simon Says
- Jack Stones
- Hopscotch

PROFILE

Blending Families, Blending Love

Walt and Leota Schoedel love their role as grandparents—and they should! They have 27 grandchildren and three great-grandchildren! Like many grandparents' families, Walt and Leota's is a blended family, each of them bringing a wonderful set of grandchildren into their new marriage.

"When Leota and I first married," Walt says, "we pledged that we would make a special effort to blend our two families. And as we look back to our 12 years together, we have been really blessed."

Walt and Leota committed to do seven things as part of their focus on blending their families and each getting to know and love their "new" grandchildren. Walt outlines their commitments this way:

1. We pray for individual families on a regular basis.
2. We host a family reunion every two years at the lake and have great times together.
3. We send our homemade birthday cards to the 11 children, their spouses, 27 grandchildren, and 3 great-grandchildren.
4. We send each a baptismal birthday card with a small gift.
5. We keep in touch via e-mail.
6. We go to sporting, theater, and musical events where they are involved, plus baptisms, birthdays, confirmations, and graduations.
7. We send a monthly calendar with birthdays and anniversary dates plus our schedule.

We play board games, cards, and Mexican Train Dominoes. We build a lot with LEGO bricks, ride bikes, play in the snow, and go to the beach. Our church has a great play zone for children 12 and under, and we are blessed to have a lot of food parks for the kids to enjoy—city, state, and national.

—Grandma Jane

Are You a Math Whiz?

Sudoku, a logical number game that involves placing numerals in a grid (9x9 spaces), is a great way to exercise your brain—and it's fun for kids, too! Check out books of Sudoku for kids at your local bookstore. Complete the puzzles together, or race each other as you each work on your own puzzle (appropriate to each skill level).

Personalize a Classic Game

Use a camera and photos, scissors, glue, dice, card stock, and markers to create a personalized version of a classic game. Design a board inspired by games like Checkers, Chutes and Ladders, Trivial Pursuit, Memory, or Candy Land. Take pictures of various family members, cut out the faces (in circles), and glue them to card stock to create game markers (or checkers). Then create your own cards (for trivia or with other game instructions), and color and design the game board. Include fun family details, like the following:

- references to favorite activities for personalized Chutes and Ladders

- pairs of family pictures (like pets, toys, cousins, aunts and uncles, and so on) for personalized Memory

- pictures (or glued-on wrappers) of favorite candy for personalized Candy Land

- trivia questions about family members or family memories for personalized Trivial Pursuit

If you're able, have the final game board and game pieces laminated. Not only will it be fun to play—it will also become a treasured keepsake for years to come.

Hit the Links, Kid Style!

Make it a tradition to take your grandchildren to a nearby miniature golf course each summer. Putt-putt courses level the playing field, often giving a rookie (or 4-year-old!) the same chance at making par as a golf-addicted grandpa!

When my grandson David was 4, he became my knight and protector. One day, I went into the upstairs bathroom at his home to take a morning shower. He wanted to come in with me to protect me from the bears. I thanked him, but told him that I would be a while and that I wanted some privacy. He agreed. I proceeded to take a rather long shower.

I had just stepped out when I heard him call from outside the door, "Are you OK, Granma?" I assured him that I was and would be out soon, to which he responded, "I just wanted to warn you about the monster in the toilet."

"Oh dear," I said, "I guess I'd better flush it quick!" (Which I did.) "Oh no, Granma, only my magic sword will do!" So I let him in to slay the monster.

—Granma Margaret P., grandmother of three

⬤ STAY CONNECTED ⟳

If you're a long-distance grandparent of a teenage or young adult grandchild, ask him to help you create a Facebook page. Once you get linked in as "friends" via Facebook, you and your grandchild can play some ongoing games together across the miles, such as Scrabulous (an online version of Scrabble) and Griddle (similar to Boggle).

Paper and Pencil Games

Your grandkids will be amazed to discover how much fun can be had with such simple and archaic supplies as a pencil and paper. Here are four easy games you can try together:

- **Dots**—Create a 10x10 or 20x20 grid of dots, and take turns drawing one line (horizontal or vertical) between two dots. Whenever a player encloses a square, that player marks it with his or her initials and takes another turn. The goal is to have the most squares at the end of the game.

- **Tic-Tac-Toe**—Create a 3x3 grid and take turns marking X's or O's until a player gets three in a row (horizontally, vertically, or diagonally).

- **Battleship**—Create two 10x10 grids, marked 1 through 10 on one axis and A through J along the other axis. Each player then draws several "boats" on his own grid (agree together on the number and size of your boats). Then take turns trying to sink each other's ships by calling out various spots on the grid (such as "B7," and so on).

- **Stickman (aka "Hangman")**—Instead of mimicking a hanging, update this game by giving it a new name like "Stickman" and simply drawing a person (without the gallows!). To play, think of a kid-friendly word or phrase and draw blanks to indicate each letter. The other player then names a letter. If that letter occurs in the word or phrase, write it in. If not, draw part of a stick-figure person. The game ends when the other player guesses the word or phrase *or* when a complete person has been drawn.

Fun With Spare Change

Save up some quarters, and then take your grandchild to an arcade. Ask your grandchild to pick a favorite game for you to try and play together. Then scout out a pinball machine and introduce him to some "old-fashioned fun"!

STAY CONNECTED

Turn the letters you write to your grandchildren into fun games by writing rebus-style messages. A rebus puzzle uses a combination of pictures (to indicate either words or sounds), plus or minus signs, and a few extra letters to create a message. Here's an example:

+R ♥ +D

Answer: You Are Loved!

As a child, I loved playing pen-and-paper games with my grandpa! We'd lie on the carpet and play for what seemed like hours. I'd always strive to beat him at Hangman! We had so much fun together ... little did I know that he was helping me learn to spell!

—Kelli, granddaughter

Traveling Trophy

Ham up your game time by selecting a really goofy trophy that can go to the winner (think white-elephant gift)! You may select something as corny as an old bowling trophy bought at a garage sale, fluorescent-green sunglasses, or a plaid, polyester jacket circa 1972. Each time you and your grandchildren play a game, the winner gets the trophy. This special prize can continue to circulate between you and your grandchildren as you play games together over the years.

Couch Potatoes No More!

Excessive video-game playing can have many negative effects, most notable of which is contributing to a sedentary, unhealthy lifestyle for kids who should be enjoying more physical exercise. In recent years, though, some new games and gaming systems involving physical activity have begun to reverse this trend— and are very popular with kids and grown-ups alike.

If your grandchild likes to play video games, join her. Games such as Dance Dance Revolution, Guitar Hero, and numerous Wii games (such as bowling, golf, tennis, and baseball) are fun to play with others and involve more physical movement than just your thumbs and fingers on a controller.

PROFILE

Once, when my grandchildren were visiting, I planned a balloon launch and backyard picnic. After we ate, I brought out four differently colored, helium-filled balloons. Each had a tag (covered in plastic) that read, "My name is Matthew" (specific to each grandchild, of course). "I live at 498 Rabbit Hole Ave., Gainesville, GA 30506. I am visiting my grandparents in New Knoxville, Ohio." The children set the balloons loose and we watched them fly until they disappeared. Matthew got an answer from people about 12 miles away. We visited them and it was great fun!

—Grandma Eileen

Out and About

Exploring the World (and All Its Adventures) With Your Grandkids

You've got a magical power.
It's the power that can transform a refrigerator box into a castle, a patch of trees into an enchanted forest, a paddleboat into a pirate ship, and a pile of blankets into Mount Everest.

It's the power of *your presence.*

Now, of course, nothing can beat those memories of time spent at Grandma's house, even if you don't live over the river and through the woods. But your grandkids will also love time with you away from your home as you take them on all sorts of outings and adventures. You can wield that magical power of yours to turn a trip down the canned goods aisle into a treasure hunt or to transform your neighborhood playground into a rocket ship to Mars. Or you can take them to explore places that have a magic of their own, like the state fair, a nature center, or the art museum. All you need to bring along is your love, your sense of adventure, and, of course, your imagination! Your presence with your grandkids is a powerful thing, and as you spend time with them indoors and out, you're leaving an indelible fingerprint on their lives. Each time, a bit of who you are is rubbing off onto who they will become.

The Best Playground Ever!

Kids love playgrounds—the slides, the swings, the monkey bars…it's heaven! So take your grandkids on a tour of playgrounds they'll never forget. Plan ahead by scouting out and identifying three to five fun playgrounds in your area; you can find them in public parks as well as elementary schools, neighborhoods, and subdivisions. When you've got your route planned, grab the picnic baskets and put together a healthy lunch.

Take your grandchildren on a hunt for "The Best Playground Ever!" Since they're the experts, they get to be the judges and will decide together which playground is the greatest. Spend a morning visiting the playgrounds and allowing about 15 to 30 minutes for the kids to play together at each one. Challenge them to try out all the play equipment at each playground. And, if you're up for it, try out some of the equipment yourself. Your grandchildren will love playing with you!

Then wrap up your morning with a picnic at the final playground. As you eat, ask your grandchildren to share:

- Which was your favorite? Why?

- Which was your least favorite? Why?

- Which slide (or swing set) did you like the best?

 BRIDGE BUILDER

Ask your grandchildren to tell you about their favorite place to play, whether it is a playground, a spot in their backyard, or at their neighbors. Then tell your grandkids about your favorite place to play as a child, such as the school playground at recess, a creek you used to make mud pies in, or the backyard of your best friend. Describe what you loved about those times.

PROFILE

Nothing beats a picnic with grandchildren in the middle of a hectic workday! Grandpa Jim remembers a time his daughter and young granddaughter met him for a picnic at a state park during his lunch break from work. "After lunch, my granddaughter Eliana and I swung on the swings together," remembers Jim. "We were right next to each other, and we held hands while we were swinging. That was very special to me!"

Spick-and-Span

Load up your grandkids in the car and go through a car wash together. Many young kids love riding in a car that is being sprayed, wiped, foamed, and rubbed by the robotic car-sized washing machine!

Or if your grandkids are older, invite them to help you wash the car. Have fun—and expect to get soaked!

An Eye for Art

Visit an art museum together and pretend you are judges at an art show as you tour the building and look at various pieces. Ahead of time, prepare a "Judge's Ballot" page for each grandchild (and yourself) that lists the following categories:

- The Most Beautiful
- The Ugliest
- The Weirdest
- The Most Real-Looking
- The One You'd Love to Hang Up in Your Bedroom

Give each grandchild a pen or pencil, and talk about the various paintings and sculptures you see as you explore the museum together, taking notes on your Judge's Ballots as you do.

At the end of the visit, sit down together and discuss your final decisions as judges for the categories on the Ballot.

If your grandchildren are about 8 years old or older, you can plan to spend an hour or more at the museum together. With grandkids who are preschool or early-elementary age, be ready to zoom through the museum, spending about 30 minutes there. Their attention span will be shorter, so keep the visit short and sweet so that they enjoy it instead of feeling bored.

Family trips are super! All 15 of us stayed in a log house in Colorado, and visited Disney World and Chicago. The key is to do them while the grandkids are young—before schedules get too busy. Families should do this if at all possible—at least once!

—Granddad Rich

6 Active Outings

Kids are full of energy! Here are six outdoor activities that will help you connect...and maybe break a sweat!

- Rent a tandem bike (a bicycle built for two) and ride it together.
- Ride a paddleboat or canoe together on a local pond or lake.
- Play hopscotch together outside.
- Play mini golf together.
- Go swimming.
- Fly a kite together.

A Blue Ribbon Day

There's no place like the state fair! A visit to the fair is a great adventure that combines fun with learning. Take a trip to the state fair with your grandchildren. While you're there, be sure to...

- *visit the animals.* Be sure to see both large animals such as cows and horses as well as smaller animals such as pigs, sheep, and rabbits.

- *watch a 4-H animal judging or award ceremony.* Throughout the fair, 4-H students' animals are being judged and awarded prizes. If your grandchildren aren't familiar with 4-H, explain to them what the 4-H kids do to raise and care for their animals. Lead them in cheering on the winners. And for fun, do some judging yourselves together, such as selecting "The Cutest Bunny" or "The Fattest Pig."

- *learn about your state's agriculture.* Look together at posters, projects, maps, and hands-on demonstrations that highlight the food and livestock produced in your state.

- *meet a farmer.* As you tour the fairgrounds, be sure to introduce your grandchildren to a farmer; you'll be sure to find adult farmers or their teenage children in or around the large animal holding areas.

- *go on a ride.*

- *learn about handicrafts.* Visit the booths or displays highlighting handicrafts such as woodworking and quilting.

- *eat something new.* State fairs are full of unique foods, from fried Twinkies to funnel cakes to farm-fresh popcorn.

Neighborhood Name Hunt

Create a unique scavenger hunt around your neighborhood (or around your house) that uses the letters of each grandchild's first name for each clue, activity, or task. For example, if your granddaughter's name is Katie, you might make up something like this:

K: Find five Hershey's **Kisses** hiding in Grandma's bedroom.

A: Stand in the backyard and (loudly) sing the **Alphabet** song.

T: Select your favorite **Toy** here at Grandma's house, and tell me why you like it.

I: Open up the freezer. You'll find a bowl with a scoop of **Ice cream** in it. Eat it!

E: Make a loud **Elephant** trumpeting sound, and then look on the back porch for a special note.

Wrap up the hunt by leading your grandchild to find a short note you've written that uses her name to emphasize that God made her unique and that she is very special to God and to you. You might write something like, "KATIE, there is no one like you in the whole world! God made you just how you are, and he loves you very much. And KATIE, I love you, too! You are my one and only KATIE, and you will always be very special to me."

Support the Home Team

Take an elementary-aged grandchild to a local high school sporting event, such as a football or basketball game or a swim meet. Eat some popcorn together and have fun cheering loudly from the stands!

PROFILE

Pork Chops on a Stick
Grandparents Steve and Kay make it a tradition to visit the Iowa State Fair every August with their grandchildren. They start early in the morning by eating cinnamon rolls together from a stand on "Main Street" in the fairgrounds. Then they tour all the animal barns: horses, cows, pigs, rabbits, and chickens. Grams (Kay) takes the kids through a tour of the exhibits in the 4-H building, and then Gramps (Steve) shows them the tractors on display and talks about the tractors he drove when he was young. The kids particularly love the petting farm where they can feed animals by hand and ride a horse. The grand finale of the day? Enjoying a state-fair delicacy together: pork chops on a stick.

Tea for Two

Plan a simple tea party for your granddaughter. If she is old enough, use a real tea set and set a fancy table, complete with a bouquet of flowers and fancy china. If your granddaughter is little, use a play tea set, but be sure to *pretend* it is very elegant and fancy! Dress up in a shirt and tie or nice dress, and invite your granddaughter to do the same. Use formal manners and model them for your granddaughter (though she may not follow suit!).

You can serve a traditional English tea, including hot tea (try yummy herbal flavors) with scones and cream or jam. Or you could select your granddaughter's favorite drink and snack, such as lemonade (in teacups!) and chocolate chip cookies.

Use the opportunity to tell your granddaughter what a lovely young woman she is, inside and out.

PROFILE

When my twin granddaughters moved six hours away, I talked with a friend of mine who was also a "long-distance grandma." She was adamant about a rule of thumb she kept: "Try hard not to let more than three months go by without seeing your grandkids in person." I've tried to keep that schedule and now I see the wisdom in what she told me—I'm not missing out on the fun stages of their growth and development.   —Grams Kay

My earliest memory is of a sidewalk tea party with Boppa. I remember the sun shining down on us as we sat together on the cement in front of his house. I remember the little lavender flowers he'd snipped and arranged in a cup to be our centerpiece. I remember the small white teacups with purple flowers painted on the outsides. And I remember the absolutely delicious water we drank elegantly together. I was only 3 years old and I hardly remember anything else from those early years—but that moment in the sun with Boppa is etched in my memory. I don't recall his words, but I do remember his smile and I distinctly remember feeling very, very special and loved.

—Kelli, granddaughter

4 Free Outings

Want to do something fun without spending money? Try these ideas:

- Visit a pet store and look at the animals.
- Visit your local fire station.
- Go to the library and visit the children's section.
- Take your grandchild fishing.

STAY CONNECTED

Even if you live far away, you can share special outings and adventures with your grandchild by taking along Teddy. First buy a special teddy bear (or other stuffed animal) for your grandchild that you will always keep at your house. This can be a special snuggle buddy for your grandchild whenever he comes to visit.

When you go on a special outing on your own, take the bear and a camera along. For example, you could take the bear to the museum with you, to a garden store, to a restaurant, to a bookstore, to the movies, or on a special vacation. Each time, pose the bear in a scenic spot and snap a photo. Then send the photo in the mail to your grandchild, telling him about your outing. He will love collecting pictures of Teddy's adventures with Grandma and Grandpa!

My best memory of my paternal grandfather was going fishing with him. He was a great teacher and was very particular about teaching us how to fish, reeling it in and even cleaning it!

—Grandma Margaret H.

Makeover at the Mall

If you have a grandchild who is a teenager (or a preteen) and you want to connect with him in a fun way, try this idea. Set aside some money from your clothing budget, and ask your grandchild to go with you to the mall and help you pick out a new outfit. Clarify that you don't want something goofy and you don't want to dress like a teenager, but you *would* like him to pick out an outfit for you that would be good for a cool grandma or grandpa. Then hit the mall!

Be a sport and try on whatever he picks out, and then let him select the final outfit for you. Once you've bought it, put it on and wear it as you eat lunch or dinner together in the food court.

 BRIDGE BUILDER

Many preteens and teenagers love to express their personality through their clothing and hairstyle choices. Sometimes these styles are not exactly what we grown-ups would prefer, but we were teenagers once, too…and our parents and grandparents probably didn't like all of our style choices either!

When you go to the mall, bring along a photograph of yourself as a teenager (or preteen) and show it to your grandchild. Laugh together about your hair or clothing, and compare it to trends today. Find something about your grandchild's outfit you can compliment, and use it to affirm his or her personality, such as, "Sarah, your earrings are very pretty. They sparkle just like you do!" or even, "Jim, I like your combat boots. They're edgy and cool—like you are."

PROFILE

Once when my son and his daughter came for a visit during a very hot summer, it suddenly got quite cold. My granddaughter only had summer clothes, so we visited garage sales and bought some long pants and tops. It was interesting to see her select exactly what she wanted among the many choices available.

—Grandma Eileen

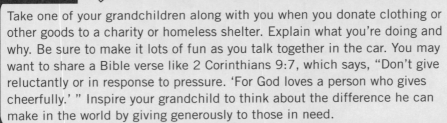

On my grandchildren's birthdays, I take each one on a birthday present shopping trip—complete with lunch! It's great fun and very revealing to learn their tastes in clothes, stores, and even food. I never knew there was a size 0 in the girls' juniors section! My granddaughter Sarah likes to order chicken salad (no onions), broccoli-cheese soup in a bread bowl, and sour apple drink for lunch at Panera Bread.

—Grandmom Hazel

PASS IT ON

Take one of your grandchildren along with you when you donate clothing or other goods to a charity or homeless shelter. Explain what you're doing and why. Be sure to make it lots of fun as you talk together in the car. You may want to share a Bible verse like 2 Corinthians 9:7, which says, "Don't give reluctantly or in response to pressure. 'For God loves a person who gives cheerfully.' " Inspire your grandchild to think about the difference he can make in the world by giving generously to those in need.

Vroom, Vroom! Zoom, Zoom!

If you have a grandchild who loves playing with cars, take him to a car show or even just on a quick tour of your local car dealership. Your grandchild will love looking at the shiny new race cars! You may want to bring along a seat so that you can take your grandchild with you on a test drive of one of the cars.

Two other great spots to visit with kids who are into vehicles are the airport and a train yard (or railroad crossing). Drive to the roof of your airport's parking structure, and then sit together on your car hood for a while and watch planes take off or land. Tour a train depot or consult a train schedule to find out when a train will be zooming by on a local railroad crossing; count the train cars together and imitate train sounds. Preschoolers, especially, will love this experience!

If your grandchild is old enough, take him to ride go-karts. Enjoy racing each other—and be sure to let your grandchild win!

A Michelangelo Moment

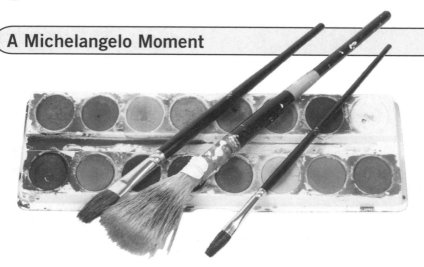

Be artists for a day! Visit a paint-your-own-pottery store with one of your grandchildren and create works of art to exchange with each other.

If you've never been to a paint-your-own-pottery store, here's how it usually works: As a customer, you select a plain pottery piece (such as a mug, a dog bowl, a picture frame, or an ornament). The store supplies you with painting supplies and ideas, and then you decorate the piece any way you'd like. A pottery expert is on hand to guide you through the process and answer questions. When you're done, the store will glaze and fire your piece and let you know when to pick it up. (Sometimes these stores charge a per-hour fee for use of supplies; others build that cost into the price of the item you select.)

PASS IT ON

As you paint pottery together, affirm your grandchild by saying something like, "Just like someone made this piece of pottery, God made you and formed you just as you are. You are very special to God—you are his work of art." You may want to share this Bible verse with your grandchild: "We are the clay, and you are the potter. We all are formed by your hand" (Isaiah 64:8).

2 Tickets, Please!

Invite your elementary school–age grandchild to attend a play with you. Community theater groups often do children's plays on a regular basis, such as renditions of fairy tales like "Snow White" or classic books like *Frog and Toad.* Or bring along upper elementary–aged children (or teenagers) to a musical. You may want to watch a film version of the musical or listen to the songs on CD ahead of time so that you are familiar with the music.

After the play, talk together about
- your favorite part.
- your favorite character.
- your favorite song.

Fun Children's Musicals and Plays to Attend
- *A Year With Frog and Toad* (musical)
- *Miss Nelson Is Missing* (musical)
- *The Adventures of Nate the Great*
- *Tales of a Fourth Grade Nothing*
- *Junie B. Jones* (musical)
- *Lily's Purple Plastic Purse*
- *Harriet the Spy*
- *Alexander and the Terrible, Horrible, No Good, Very Bad Day* (musical)
- *If You Give a Mouse a Cookie*

Back in Time
Visit a history museum with your grandchild. At the end of your visit, talk about this question: "If you could pick any time in history in which to live—besides the time we're in now—which would you pick? Why?"

I appreciate the one-on-one experiences with my grandchildren more than the crowded events. I like to take them one at a time to some place either by myself or with their grandmother—or share an experience by attending and watching something together. We've had great fishing moments and planned birthday bashes eating out at a restaurant of their choice (often McDonald's).

—Grandpa Charles

One time my grandma and grandpa took me by myself to visit my aunt Susie. They picked me up at my house, and we drove first to Uncle Max's house. Aunt RoseAnn let me play with all her paper dolls.

I went on a tractor ride with Grandpa and Uncle Max. We rode all over the farm and I saw cornfields. The dog came with us, but he was kind of shy. He tried to jump off the tractor! We rode through some woods and then turned around and came back.

Then, we left their house and stopped to get me an ice cream cone on the way to Aunt Susie's house. When we got there, we swam in her pool. The dogs tried to get in the pool with us! After that, we ate dinner and after dinner I went to bed.

I couldn't fall asleep, so I kept watching the adults out the window. Then I decided I was hungry, so I went downstairs and Grandma got me some grapes and I got to stay up another half hour. I went back to bed, but I kept rolling off the bed in my sleep. I woke up in the morning and we had waffles for breakfast, swam in the pool, and came back home.

It was very fun to go somewhere with Grandma and Grandpa myself. I wanted to hug them a million times.

—Maddie, granddaughter (age 6)

PROFILE

Pirate's Treasure!
Four-year-old Davis will never forget the amazing pirate's treasure he found in the backyard of "Pawky" and "Ammy's" house during a summertime visit. When he was exploring in the backyard with Pawky, they found an old treasure map hidden away. Along with a rough sketch, they found a note and instructions from a pirate named Happy Jack who'd shipwrecked there years ago. (Davis was too young to wonder why a pirate ship would have wrecked in the middle of Mississippi!)

With the help of the entire family, Davis trekked through the backyard, making all sorts of twists and turns. Along the way, he found an old pirate flag and some remnants of the shipwreck—wooden boards and glass bottles. Eventually, he found the buried treasure, a box filled with a few toy cars. It was an adventure he'll never forget!

I remember a time my grandson and I were sitting on our swinging bench in the backyard and just "being" together. After a while, we picked sweet clovers and I taught him how to braid the clovers to make a crown and bracelet for his mom. I think that it was so special for me because as a child I loved braiding sweet clover!

—Grams Jeanne

Naturalists for a Day

Visit a nature center, wildlife preserve, or local pond with your grandchildren and pretend to be naturalists; bring along blank paper, pencils or crayons, magnifying glasses, and a disposable camera. Take time together to observe the plants and animals you see. You may want to

- create a list of every animal and insect you see during your time together.

- make a sketch of a bird, insect, or flower you find.

- get on your hands and knees to look for tiny creatures like ants or beetles. (You could also lift up rocks and look underneath for worms, beetles, and pill bugs.)

- help your grandchilden take photographs of their favorite plants and trees, animals, and insects.

At the end of your time together, talk about the neat things you observed and affirm your grandchildren for their good work as naturalists!

PROFILE

We took our twin granddaughters to a catch-and-release pond for their first experience fishing. I had to show them how to hook the worm and then cast the line. The first fish caught brought delighted squeals from both girls, and their eyes just sparkled. I explained why we released them back into their home instead of eating them.

It is always so refreshing to see the world anew from a youngster's eyes and what they say about the world around them. It keeps me young and continually reminds me how God's world is awesome.   —Gramps Steve

As you look together at the wonders of nature, draw your grandchildren's attention to God's amazing creativity. Point out the small wonders we often pass by without noticing and give God the credit for his artistry. For example, you might say, "Look at the tiny veins in that leaf. Isn't it awesome how God designed it so beautifully?" or "Look at the beautiful bright-red color God made the cardinal!"

You might also want to share this Bible verse: "You will live in joy and peace. The mountains and hills will burst into song, and the trees of the field will clap their hands!" (Isaiah 55:12). You can talk to your grandchildren about how all of nature praises God in its own way, and you could look for examples of this, such as a beautiful flower opening toward the sun, a bird singing a lovely tune, or the peaceful flow of a gentle breeze.

6 Ideas for Winter Fun

When it's cold and snowy, you can still have fun. Try these ideas with your grandkids:

- Take them for a drive at night to see houses decorated with Christmas lights.

- Build a snowman together.

- Take them sledding.

- Fill up a spray bottle with water and food coloring, and then bundle up and "spray paint" snow together.

- Visit a Christmas tree farm.

- Make homemade instant hot chai mix (see page 73) and deliver it to friends and neighbors.

Pops Bob has great childhood memories of his own grandfather. "I loved going fishing with Grampy," he says. But even more memorable was the scandal Grampy caused during one fishing excursion: "He let me set off fireworks with him!" Bob explains. Other great memories for Bob were the times Grampy took him mushroom hunting. "It was so boring to me as a kid, but at the same time I really loved it!" Bob learned patience and a love of the outdoors during those long, relatively uneventful mushroom-hunting trips; they were times he now treasures as an adult.

Down on the Farm

Make arrangements with a local farm to visit it with your grandchildren and get a quick tour. Look at the various animals and, if your grandchildren are young, imitate their sounds together. Ask the farmer to show you his or her tractor or other farm equipment. Talk with your grandchildren about how food is produced; after all, it doesn't come from the grocery store or the drive-through window!

Or find an orchard or U-pick farm you can visit, such as an apple orchard, a strawberry patch, a pumpkin patch, or a CSA (Community Supported Agriculture) farm that allows customers to harvest their own veggies. Pick some fruit or vegetables together. Then, if you're up for it, make something from them when you get home, such as chocolate-dipped strawberries, spiced pumpkin seeds, or applesauce. (See page 70 for instructions for making homemade applesauce or page 72 for a recipe for spiced pumpkin seeds.)

CHECK IT OUT

To locate a family farm nearby, go to www.localharvest.org. There you'll find listings of farms with descriptions of their produce and contact information. Contact the farm to find out about visiting hours; many family farmers will arrange a tour of their farm for young kids. If the farmer doesn't charge a fee, consider thanking him by purchasing some eggs, veggies, or other produce.

🌉 BRIDGE BUILDER

Have fun answering silly questions together, such as

- If you were an animal living on a farm, what animal would you want to be? Why?

- Let's pretend we own a dairy farm and we got to make our own ice cream. What kinds of flavors would we want to make? Let's think of some that no one else has made before!

- What's the best vegetable in the world? What's the worst?

- Imagine you were a farmer. What do you think you'd like about it? What would be tough about it?

- Let's make up names for the animals we saw today. What would you call [describe an animal you saw]? Why?

During the summer, I spent hours at Grandmother's house. She was never too busy to let me wander around the farm with her, doing whatever she did. We helped gather eggs while they were still warm. Her calloused hands would nimbly reach underneath each Rhode Island Red to pluck still-warm eggs from the nest; then she would gently lay them in her apron, held securely with the free hand. Grandmother made me an apron once. I never got the hang of holding it just right so the eggs were safe, but she let me try. With corn shuck brooms (a long one for her—a smaller one for me), she taught me how to sweep the hard, dirt-packed backyard until it was free of leaves and branches.

—Elizabeth, granddaughter

Sunny Day Supplies

Keep these supplies on hand for fun outdoors with preschool-aged grandkids:

- Paintbrush and bucket (for painting with water)
- Sidewalk chalk
- Tennis ball
- Bubble mix
- Inflatable beach ball
- Some heavy objects and light, buoyant objects (to play "sink or float" in a bucket of water)
- Small Frisbee
- Large beach towel (for sitting on)
- Sunscreen
- Children's hat and sunglasses

STAY CONNECTED

If you don't live near your granddaughter, you can send your preteen or teenage granddaughter a "Girlfriends Party" in the mail! For about $10, you can buy an inexpensive nail polish, a small bottle of hand lotion, and a small bottle of bubble bath. Make a tiny baggie of homemade bath salts, too. Then use pretty stationery to write a short note to your granddaughter, telling her that she is beautiful inside and out. Put it all together in a box and ship it off.

Patriotic Parade

Go to a patriotic parade with your grandchildren on Veterans Day, Memorial Day, or the Fourth of July. If you're a veteran or if your parents or grandparents were veterans, tell your grandchildren about it. Share with them what it means to you to live in this country; talk about the honor of serving the country as a member of the armed forces.

Indoor "Outings" for Rainy Days

Trail to a Treat

Use sticky notes to lead your grandchildren on a trail through your house. Number the notes 1 through 10, and then, on the front of each note, write a short clue that leads to the next note. For example, "Look in the shower," or "Open the dictionary," or "Look under Grandpa's shoes."

Then, on the back side of the notes, write words or letters that will create a message once they've collected all the notes and put them in order. For example, "Want some C O O K I E S ?"

Once you've got the notes prepared, plant them around your house using the clues you've written.

When your grandkids arrive, lead them to the first note and go on the hunt together. (Make sure they work together as they find the various clues.)

At the end of the hunt, see if they discover the secret message on the back on their own; if not, prompt them to look on the back of the notes for their final clue. Then wrap up the game with a delicious treat of cookies and milk!

Whenever one of our granddaughters turns about 8, she gets a trip by herself with us to the American Girl Place in Chicago. We buy her a doll (she gets only one and is able to choose the one she wants), and we provide a little money for her to carefully select something to go with her doll. One granddaughter picked a T-shirt, another an outfit, and another chose animals. We walk The Magnificent Mile down Michigan Avenue since Grandma is too cheap to park too close!

—Grandma Jane

Girlfriends Party

Plan a special grandmother-granddaughter girls night. Select some of these activities to do together:

- Go to a store and buy silly slippers together that you can wear during the Girlfriends Party.

- Wear comfy PJs.

- Paint each other's toenails.

- Make scented bath salts together (see page 23 for instructions).

- Fix each other's hair.

- Do a facial mask together.

- Watch a kid-friendly "chick flick" together such as a *Dora the Explorer* video (preschool), *The Little Mermaid* (early elementary), or *Anne of Green Gables* (late elementary or older).

- Make and eat a yummy snack together, such as brownies, Pizookies (see page 74) or Rice Krispies treats (see page 68).

Use every opportunity you can during the evening to affirm and encourage your granddaughter. As you enjoy doing beauty treatments together (fixing hair, painting nails, and so on), draw the focus to your granddaughter's *inner beauty,* affirming character traits such as her kindness, creativity, joyfulness, and enthusiasm.

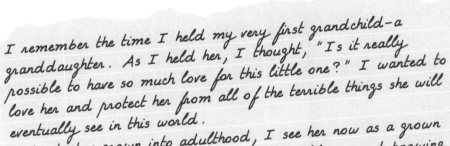

I remember the time I held my very first grandchild—a granddaughter. As I held her, I thought, "Is it really possible to have so much love for this little one?" I wanted to love her and protect her from all of the terrible things she will eventually see in this world.

As she has grown into adulthood, I see her now as a grown woman, striving to be a good mother herself now and knowing it won't be easy. I try to reassure her—and all of my grandchildren—that no matter what problems they may face in this life, there is a God who loves them deeply and who wants them to be with him someday.

—Grandpa Fred

Camping...Without Mosquitoes!

Have an indoor camping trip with your grandchildren in your family room or basement. Here are some ideas of things you can do:

- Create an indoor tent by draping sheets over the dining room table.

- Sleep on the floor in sleeping bags.

- Use flashlights to explore the house in the dark.

- Eat campout food for dinner, such as hot dogs or foil dinners (cooked in the oven).

- Make s'mores in the microwave. (Just put chocolate and a marshmallow on a graham cracker and microwave it for 10 seconds. Check it to see if it's ready. If not, repeat for 10 seconds and check again. Continue until it's just right.)

- Sit around an imaginary campfire and sing the "Going on a Bear Hunt" song together. (You can find the words at www.dltk-kids.com/crafts/teddy/bearhunt.html.)

- Read a bedtime story with flashlights.

Keep up the camping theme in the morning by pretending you're outdoors. You could say things like, "I love the smell of fresh pine trees!" or "Can you hear those birds singing?" Then serve a camping trip breakfast such as bacon and scrambled eggs or cereal and milk eaten around the make-believe campfire.

Yum, Yum

Cooking and Eating Together

Many family memories are centered around celebrations and shared meals—the Thanksgiving where two siblings conspired to see if the canned whipped cream could squirt from the table to the ceiling (it did); the potluck where you secretly figured out what Great-Aunt Esmiralda brought so you could avoid it (since all her food tasted like mothballs); and the birthday where the baking powder in the homemade cake was accidentally replaced with baking soda.

See, it doesn't require a chef to create a good memory about food—though some memories may be best relived later!

Many grandchildren tell great, almost mythic, stories about their grandmother's cooking. But even if you can hardly make toast, you won't find this chapter daunting. If you can't cook, there are plenty of ways you can learn how to cook alongside your grandchild. And if you can cook, there are plenty of skills you can teach.

What's most important, though, is that you spend time with your grandchild doing the daily activities of life—the "quotidian mysteries," as some call them. Doing the dishes or rolling out pie crust is a great time to discuss the joys and trials of life. God is with us in whatever we do, and food is a great gift from God to be shared in all sorts of ways.

So, grab an apron, open the cupboard, and start cooking!

WARNING

Be aware that some children have food allergies that can be dangerous. Be sure parents provide you with information about allergies their children may have, and be sure to carefully read food labels. Hidden ingredients may cause allergy-related problems. Also, to avoid choking hazards, be sure that the food you select is appropriate for the age and chewing abilities of your grandchild.

We're sure you know all this: after all, you're a super grandparent!

With our grandchildren we've planted spring flowers, gotten very dirty, found surprise worms and roly-poly bugs under rocks, and sung as we gardened.

—Grandmom Hazel

How Does Your Garden Grow?

In early spring, plan a vegetable garden with your grandchild. Select seeds from a seed catalog or garden store, start them inside, and set them in the soil you've prepared once the chance of frost has passed. (Allow your grandchild to help you prepare the soil with a child-sized shovel or hoe.)

Plan a weekly (or biweekly) date to care for the garden together. you're an avid gardener and have a large plot, you may want to set aside several square feet for your grandchild to tend, while you remain responsible for the rest.

When it's time to harvest the crop, pick and prepare the vegetables together. Eat them the day you harvest them, if possible. Consider saving the seeds (learn how at www.seedsave.org) so that next year you can plant seeds from the same crop.

When you eat the vegetables grown in your yard, teach your grandchild a traditional hymn of thankfulness such as "We Gather Together" or "Now Thank We All Our God."

 BRIDGEBUILDER

Ask your grandchild about his experience gardening. What did he like best? worst? If you have one, tell a story about your experiences of gardening as a child or adult. What have you planted that's grown well? What has failed? What are you the most proud of? What do you like about growing your own food? Does gardening make you feel closer to God?

PASS IT ON

Read part of the story of Creation in Genesis 1 and 2 (suggested text: Genesis 1:24-31). How can gardening help fulfill God's instruction to the world in this chapter?

If your grandchild lives far away and has a bit of earth at her home, make and send a garden kit. Include seeds that would grow well in her location, a small shovel, a watering can, and your own list of gardening tips and instructions. If your grandchild lives in an apartment or condo, send a lightweight pot with bagged soil and herb seeds. Include instructions on how to plant and use the herbs—and maybe even a recipe or two.

Cook Together!

Once your grandchild can walk and has small motor and some communication skills, he can cook with you. Pull up a chair (or get a special stool) for your grandchild to stand on so he can reach the counter and mix, stir, or knead. You can make special things together or just cook what you normally cook, with your grandchild helping where he can. To him, it won't be normal, it will be fun to cook with grandpa!

Here's a list of easy-to-prepare foods you can teach your grandchild how to make:

- Peanut butter and jelly sandwiches
- Grilled cheese sandwiches (Help with the grilling!)
- Lemonade (Let your grandchild help roll the lemons on the table or floor before they're washed and squeezed.)
- Cinnamon toast
- Cream cheese and sunflower seed sandwiches
- Ants on a log (Spread peanut butter or cream cheese in celery and top it with raisins.)

Christmas Cooking

For Christmas, make a gingerbread house together. You can purchase a kit, make one the old-fashioned way, or "cheat" by first making a cardboard house with masking tape and then using frosting "paste" to place graham crackers all over the structure. Decorate with all sorts of candies, licorice, and marshmallows.

Pretend Food

Many young children have pretend food made from plastic, wood, or cloth that they play with. As a gift idea—if your grandchild doesn't have any—consider making or purchasing some. When you give the pretend food to your grandchild, plan on playing "food" with them. Prepare outrageous food combinations together and "serve" them to your family.

Remembering Grandma's Cooking

Grandma always had a lot of food in her house. Before Christmas she would cook for a couple of weeks in preparation for our big family. After the feast, she would pull out all kinds of snacks—popcorn, trail mix, and bars just in case we got hungry. In a back room, she often had soft rolls.

—Ben, grandson

Mayonnaise sandwiches were one of my favorite treats at Grandmother's house, since Mother never let us have them at home.

—Elizabeth, mother and granddaughter

When I was invited to visit Grandpa and Grandma for lunch, my grandma (who seldom said anything) would bake a lemon pie for me—even though I don't particularly like lemon pies. I understood that lemon pie was her language of love.

—Grandpa Charles

Sharing Recipes

For years, families have passed down recipes from one generation to the next. Here are several ways you can do it:

- Teach your grandchild how to make a traditional family dish. Prepare the dish together, and write out the recipe so she can make it on her own at home. Consider making it a tradition (for instance, Grandma and Amy always make the Thanksgiving stuffing together).

- Make your grandchild a personalized recipe box. Recipe boxes are available for purchase at many stores, or you can just get a regular card file. Make dividers for the box based on family members' favorite foods: "Amy's favorites," "Grandpa's favorites," "from Great-grandma," and so on. Write out family recipes on cards—by hand—and send recipes with birthday or holiday cards in the mail.

- Consider making a cookbook. There are a variety of online resources to help you and your grandchild create and publish your own cookbook. Or you can simply type out recipes, copy them, and put them in three-ring binders.

Write and Publish Your Own Cookbook
- www.familycookbookproject.com
- www.heritagecookbook.com
- www.platefullofmemories.com

Cookbook With Footnotes
Give your grandchild your favorite cookbook—or a copy of it if you can find one. Make notes in the cookbook—when you tried a recipe, who liked it, and hints for improvements or substitutions. If you're giving your original copy, there are probably notes in there already, but it doesn't hurt to add more. If it's a different copy, replicate your notes into the cookbook for your grandchild. It's fun to know when someone else tried something, what they thought, and how it turned out.

☞ CHECK IT OUT
Recommended Cookbooks for Children

- *Pretend Soup and Other Real Recipes: A Cookbook for Preschoolers & Up* by Mollie Katzen and Ann Henderson (10 Speed Press). This book and *Salad People,* below, teach young children how to cook through illustrations. The books also include written instructions for the adults. Healthy, fun foods.

- *Salad People and More Real Recipes: A New Cookbook for Preschoolers & Up* by Mollie Katzen (10 Speed Press)

- *Honest Pretzels and 64 Other Amazing Recipes for Cooks Ages 8 & Up* by Mollie Katzen (10 Speed Press)

One Christmas, my mother compiled all of my grandmother's recipes into a family recipe book. She gave each grandchild a copy, with a special note from Grandmama in the front of each one. The book has family photographs in it, as well as Grandmama's notes on each of the recipes. I treasure this book and the family and food history it represents.

—Joy, granddaughter

Grandkids love milkshakes! All you need is plenty of ice cream, milk, and chocolate. Mix and eat. Do this over and over for years and you'll become the milkshake queen!

—Carolyn, grandmother of 11

- *Simply in Season Children's Cookbook* by Mark Beach and Julie Kauffman (Herald Press). Based on the Mennonite Central Committee's popular cookbook *Simply in Season,* the children's edition has simple, healthy recipes that call for seasonal ingredients. A great book to accompany a garden or a trip to the farmers' market. For ages 6 and up.
- *Betty Crocker's Cook Book for Boys and Girls* (1957 edition, still in print). Though the recipes are more about assemblage than cooking, this is a fun book that will bring back many memories for a grandparent to share with his grandchild. Great retro illustrations and photographs!

Mish-Mash-Smash Guacamole

Guacamole can be quick and easy to make—and it's full of great vitamins for adventurous grandkids who like to eat mushy green stuff! You can vary this recipe to fit your tastes, but here are the basic ratios:

2 ripe avocados (The avocados should be brown on the outside, bright green on the inside, and firm but with just a little give. If they mush when you squeeze them slightly, they are too ripe; if they don't give at all, put them in a brown paper bag for a day to let them ripen more.)
2 Roma tomatoes
½ small red onion
cilantro to taste

(Optional: Add one mild Anaheim pepper, seeded and chopped; Anaheims are much less spicy than traditional jalapeños.)

With your grandchild, chop the avocados into 1- to 2-inch pieces (or even bigger); chop or dice the remaining ingredients and place them all in a bowl. Sprinkle with just a bit of salt and pepper, drizzle with some olive oil, and then squeeze half of a freshly cut lime over the mix. Toss the ingredients and then use a potato masher or a fork to "mish-mash-smash" everything to the consistency you want, keeping things a bit chunky. Taste and adjust seasoning to your liking, and then eat with tortilla chips. If the guacamole won't be eaten immediately, squeeze more lime juice over the top of it to prevent browning.

Restaurant Date

Take your grandchild to a restaurant—either your favorite or his favorite. Order your favorite dishes and give each other a taste.

☞ CHECK IT OUT

Keep these healthy, simple foods around the house when your grandchildren come for a visit:

- peanut or other nut butters
- graham crackers
- apples
- carrots
- raisins
- cheese (Cut into squares and serve with the raisins.)
- juice and milk

I love to bake cookies with my grandma. We cut out cookies using different cookie cutters depending on the season. Grandma bakes them while my sisters, cousins, and I stir the frosting and get out sprinkles.

When the cookies are done, we frost them. We use green for Christmas; pink, purple, and yellow for Easter; red, white, and blue for the Fourth of July; and we use every single color of the rainbow in between holidays. After the cookies are frosted, we put LOTS of sprinkles on the cookies. On some of the cookies we only put a few sprinkles because Grandpa likes them that way. My little sister and little cousin usually eat all the frosting off their cookies as they decorate.

When we are finished, everyone eats one cookie and saves the rest for after dinner. My little sister and little cousin have their own special plate of cookies because no one wants to eat the ones they make since they lick their fingers. By the end we have made a big mess, so we help Grandma clean up by wiping down the counter and doing the dishes.

—Grace, granddaughter (age 8)

PASS IT ON

Thankfulness

During mealtime, discuss what it means to be thankful for the food God has provided us. Read 1 Timothy 6:6-8 together and discuss the following questions:

- How can we show our thankfulness for food to God and others?
- What does it mean to have "enough" food? clothes?
- Why do we forget to be thankful? How could we better remember?

After your discussion, pray together and sing a chorus of thanks, such as the "Doxology."

8 Variations on an Easy Classic

Rice Krispies treats are a favorite across generations. Use the recipe on the box, but add these mix-ins to create your own unique treats with your grandchild!

- *Swirl Treats:* Divide the marshmallows and butter in half, and melt them in two pans simultaneously. Add a few drops of food coloring to each mix to create two different shades. Mix the Rice Krispies (halved) into each color, and then use spoons to press various sizes of glops and dollops together into one large pan to cool.

- *Chocolate Lovers Treats:* Mix Cocoa Krispies with the Rice Krispies to total the required amount. At the end of the recipe, sprinkle chocolate chips on top and press them into the treats while they're still warm.

- *Rocky Road:* Follow the Chocolate Lovers directions above, but mix in some mini marshmallows and nuts by hand when the concoction has cooled enough to touch.

- *Rainbow Krispies:* Add rainbow sprinkles to the mix right before you press it into the pan to cool; the colors will bleed onto the treats adding rainbow-colored spots.

- *Fruity Treats:* Chop dried fruits (like apricots, apples, and cherries) and mix them in when the treat mix is cooled sufficiently to handle.

- *Breakfast Mix-up:* Select two other breakfast cereals to include in the treats, such as Cheerios and Kix. Mix them with the Rice Krispies, being sure to still measure the total amount of cereal required by the recipe.

- *Snowballs:* Carefully melt some white chocolate chips in the microwave or a double boiler. When the Rice Krispies mixture is ready to cool, butter up your hands and form balls or mounds and place on waxed paper. Then drizzle each ball with melted white chocolate.

- *Krispie Friends:* Press the mixture onto wax paper and quickly use gingerbread-people cookie cutters to form people-shaped treats.

I think my paternal grandmother is one of the most creative women I have ever known. When I was a child she would plan unusual parties for us. At one picnic each grandchild got a shoe box with a random lunch she had packed, such as a lemon, yogurt, a banana, and a sandwich. We all wanted to see what other people had received.

—Liebe, granddaughter

Box Lunch Spectacular

For an outing with your grandchildren (or even a special lunch inside), plan a box lunch spectacular. Here's what you do:

1. Gather shoe boxes so that each person participating will have one.

2. Put a different lunch into each shoe box. For instance, in the first box, place a peanut butter jelly sandwich, an apple, ants on a log, a chocolate chip cookie, and a can of soda. In the second box, place a cheese sandwich, an orange, carrot sticks, a pudding cup, and a juice box. The brilliant thing about box lunches is that you can use what you have around the house without having to purchase special ingredients.

3. Consider adding a "joke" item to each box. "Jokes" include an empty ice cream cone or a lemon or lime.

4. Once the boxes are prepared, cover them and write a number ("1," "2," "3," and so on) on each one.

5. When it's time to eat, write each number on a piece of paper and have your grandchildren draw a number. They each get the corresponding mystery box.

The rules? No complaining, but kind trading is allowed.

You can use this same idea for leftovers. Prepare different mystery plates, give them numbers, and serve up a fun leftover dinner!

TIP

This is a great multigenerational activity. If your group is rather large, arrange for other family members to bring box lunches to the event, too.

Lost Arts

Teach your older grandchild a new, more complex food preparation skill. This could include baking bread, canning tomatoes, canning jam or jelly, making applesauce, preparing pickles, making sauerkraut, baking a cake from scratch, or making ketchup.

If your grandchild enjoys the process (and end result!), start looking for the supplies she would need to do this on her own. You can find canning jars, food mills, and large pots at thrift and antique stores. These would make great, meaningful gifts.

Applesauce

For this recipe, try a combination of several of the following apples: Braeburn, Pink Lady, Granny Smith, or McIntosh. Avoid Red Delicious!

8 cups cubed and peeled apples
½ cup packed brown sugar
(optional)
2 teaspoons grated lemon rind

3 tablespoons lemon juice
1 teaspoon ground cinnamon
1 teaspoon vanilla extract
dash of salt

Combine ingredients in a Dutch oven or large covered pan over medium heat. Cook 25 minutes or until apples are tender, stirring occasionally. Remove from heat and mash with a potato masher. Serve warm, or refrigerate. This recipe may also be frozen.

Eat Your Heritage

Teach your grandchild how to prepare food that hearkens back to your family history. Don't know how to cook foods from your family heritage? Explore the Internet or a good bookstore together to find appropriate recipes. Together, prepare an ethnic meal or snack for your family. Include appropriate decorations such as flags, national flowers, and appropriate dress.

STAY CONNECTED

Send your child a cookbook or collection of recipes that reflect your family heritage. Include notes or stories, if you can, about how your ancestors prepared and ate food.

Read Acts 2:46-47 with your grandchild: "They worshiped together at the Temple each day, met in homes for the Lord's Supper, and shared their meals with great joy and generosity—all the while praising God and enjoying the goodwill of all the people. And each day the Lord added to their fellowship those who were being saved." Explain that this verse is about the early church. Discuss the following questions together:

- Can we worship God through our eating?
- What does it mean to share food with "great joy and generosity"?

 BRIDGE BUILDER

Discuss your family background with your grandchild. Ask her: "What do you know about our family? What do you wish you knew?" Use this opportunity to share about your experiences of being in your family. What makes your family unique? What traits and values do you all share?

What Would You Like to Order?

Invite your young grandchild to help you create a restaurant. Ahead of time (over the phone), decide on the food you'd like to serve, and then purchase and prepare the ingredients. When your grandchild arrives, create menus together, set the table, decorate the room, select background music, don aprons and chef hats, and get out some play money. Then invite your grandchild's parents and siblings to come over for the meal while the two of you serve as waiters, cooks, and cashiers. Be sure to take pictures—this is a memory you'll want to keep!

> *I remember Grandmama's poundcake. She loved baking cakes and always seemed to have one when we would visit. I liked the dense, sweet cake and I savored the caramel icing that she had generously poured over the top. Many times I would carefully leave the slabs of icing until last.*
>
> —Liebe, granddaughter

The Gift of Food

Food always makes a useful and thoughtful gift. Here are some great recipes you and your grandchild can make together to give to family and friends for Christmas, birthdays, or just because.

Recipes

Spiced Pumpkin Seeds

Seeds from 2 medium pumpkins, or several winter squashes (such as butternut, acorn, delicata, or carnival)

1 tablespoon olive oil
1 teaspoon celery salt
1 teaspoon ground cumin

Heat oven to 300 degrees. Remove the seeds from the pumpkin or squash. Discard the pulp. Spread the seeds evenly on an ungreased baking sheet. Bake until dried, about 1 hour. Toss the seeds with the rest of the ingredients in a large skillet. Cook, stirring occasionally, until the seeds are lightly toasted, about 3 minutes.

Hummus

Hummus is a Middle Eastern dip made of chickpeas and tahini (sesame seed butter).

2 cans garbanzo beans, drained (chickpeas)
¼ cup tahini (You can find it in the Middle Eastern section of the grocery store.)
2 cloves garlic
2 tablespoons lemon juice
¾ teaspoon ground coriander
salt to taste
½ teaspoon ground cumin seeds
¼–½ teaspoon cayenne pepper

In a food processor (or blender, if you don't have a processor), purée all ingredients together. Taste and adjust seasonings. Put in a container to give away with a bag of chips, or have it for a snack or appetizer with tortilla or pita chips or chopped raw vegetables. It also makes a great lunch or dinner served in pita bread with lettuce, tomatoes, cucumber, olives, and feta cheese.

At my Grandmama's house, each of us had a mug with our name on it. When we would get together, we would each drink hot chocolate (or coffee, for the adults) from our special mug. It was fun to see them hanging in a row when they weren't in use!

—Joy, granddaughter

Hot Drink Mixes

Friendship Tea

2½ cups Tang or orange drink
  powder
1½ cups sugar
12 ounces instant lemonade mix
  (sweetened)
1½ cups lemon-flavored tea
2 teaspoons ground cloves
2 teaspoons ground cinnamon
1 teaspoon ground nutmeg

Mix together. To serve, add 2 tablespoons to a cup of very hot water.

Instant Chai Mix

1 cup nondairy creamer
1 cup French vanilla–flavored
  nondairy creamer
1 cup instant tea (unsweetened)
2½ cups sugar
1 teaspoon ground cardamom
1 teaspoon ground cloves
2 teaspoons ground ginger
2 teaspoons ground cinnamon

Mix together. If desired, use a blender to grind 1 cup at a time into a very fine powder. To serve, add 2 heaping teaspoons to a cup of very hot water.

Fun Desserts to Give or Keep

Peanut Butter Cereal Bars

1 cup white sugar
1 cup white corn syrup
1 cup creamy peanut butter
7-8 cups puffed rice cereal
1-2 cups chocolate chips

Heat sugar and corn syrup in a very large saucepan on low heat until dissolved. Do not boil. Add peanut butter and cereal. Stir until mixed. Immediately spread into a buttered 9x13 pan. Sprinkle chocolate chips on top. Cover for a few minutes to allow chocolate chips to melt. Spread like frosting using a knife. Let cool and cut into squares.

Pizookies

1 cup unsalted butter
2¼ cups flour
1 teaspoon salt
1 teaspoon baking soda
¼ cup sugar
1¼ cups brown sugar
1 egg
1 egg yolk
2 tablespoons milk
1½ teaspoons vanilla extract
1 cup semisweet chocolate chips
vanilla ice cream (optional)

Preheat oven to 375 degrees. Melt the butter in a saucepan over low heat. Sift together the flour, salt, and baking soda. Set aside. Pour the melted butter in a large bowl. Add the sugar and brown sugar. Cream the butter and sugars with an electric mixer on medium speed. Add the egg, egg yolk, milk, and vanilla extract to the sugar-butter mixture. Mix. Slowly incorporate the flour mixture until thoroughly combined. Stir in the chocolate chips (these can be omitted or increased depending on taste). Scoop onto baking sheets, 6 cookies per sheet, or spread dough on the bottom of four 9-inch pie tins. Bake for 15 minutes or until golden brown. Serve cookies or cool and store. Pizookies are best topped with vanilla ice cream and served warm.

Sand Art Cookie Mix

Layer ingredients in this order in a glass quart jar:
⅓ cup cocoa
⅔ cup sugar
½ cup chocolate chips
½ cup vanilla chips
⅔ cup brown sugar
1⅛ cups flour mixed with ½ teaspoon soda and ½ teaspoon salt
½ cup chopped walnuts or pecans (optional)

Put the following label on the jar:
"Combine jar ingredients with 1 teaspoon vanilla, ⅔ cup oil, and 3 eggs. Bake at 350 degrees for 18–20 minutes in a greased 9x13 pan."

Feed Others

With your grandchild, volunteer to help at a local food bank or homeless shelter feeding or preparing food for people who are hungry. A great resource for finding local food banks is www.secondharvest.org. You can also Google "food bank" and your city name to find organizations in your area. Use this time as an opportunity to show your grandchild what it means to give of yourself to others.

 BRIDGE BUILDER

Discuss this question with your grandchild: "Have you ever been truly hungry?" What does it mean to be hungry? Does it mean that your stomach growls? What does it signify when we say, "I'm starving." Are we really starving? What does that say about people who are truly hungry?

Tell stories about times you interacted with people who truly have experienced hunger. How did you feel?

PASS IT ON

Memorize Proverbs 22:9, "Blessed are those who are generous, because they feed the poor," with your grandchild. Talk about God's love and concern for the poor and how we are called to care for them.

Storytelling: Your Story + Their Story = God's Story

Storytelling Tips and Ideas

What do you think of when you hear the word *story*? Do you remember times around the campfire listening to ghost stories? Do you recall missionary week at your church and the surprising tales missionaries told of the ways God was working throughout the world? Do you recollect the first Bible storybook you ever read aloud to your children or grandchildren?

As Christians, our lives are centered around a story—the story of God's creation of humanity, humanity's fall into sin, and Christ's work of redemption. Without this story, our faith would not exist. And even within our own personal histories—singing songs in Sunday school, a youthful time of rebellion, or a surprise experience of grace—we can see God's hands at work.

One of the most important roles of a grandparent is that of storyteller—telling the stories that, without you, would be lost. In this chapter you'll find a variety of ideas for storytelling—from the overtly spiritual to the extraordinarily silly. But within each storytelling activity is an opportunity to create meaningful memories and model ways of living that glorify God and love others.

In my interactions and activities with my grandchildren, I try to follow this guideline for all I do: Connect my story, God's story, and their story.

—Walt, grandfather of 27 and great-grandfather of three

Interviewing: Asking, Telling, and Listening

One of the best ways to learn about someone is to interview her. Suggest to your grandchild that each of you interview each other. Set a time and prepare by putting together several questions.

Before you start, review the following ground rules for the interviews:

1. Avoid interrupting! The interviewer should ask questions and then listen to the interviewee answer them.

2. No commentary. An interview is not the time to agree or disagree with someone. It's simply a time to ask, tell, and listen.

3. Have fun! The purpose of this interview is to learn about each other, not make a good grade or impress anyone. This is the most important rule of all!

☞ CHECK IT OUT

If you and your grandchild decide to interview each other, check out the resources on www.storycorps.net. StoryCorps is a not-for-profit program that seeks "to honor and celebrate one another's lives through listening." StoryCorps has a mobile recording booth (a StoryBooth) that travels throughout the United States, giving people the opportunity to interview one another, recording the interview, giving the participants a CD of their recording, and placing another recording in the Library of Congress. Whether you're able to officially be part of StoryCorps through a recorded interview or not, StoryCorps' website contains a gold mine of interview questions that you can use in your own conversation with your grandchild. Just click on the link to the "Great Questions" page.

Questions to Ask

Here are some questions to ask when interviewing each other. Don't forget to make some up on your own!

- What's your first memory?
- What's the time you laughed the hardest? cried the hardest?
- What's your most valuable possession? Why?
- What's your favorite book/movie/song/food? Why? What memories do you have associated with this?
- What has been the happiest moment of your life so far?
- What did you do for someone else today/this week/this month?
- Have you ever been to camp? Did you like it? What happened?

- What do/did you like the most about school or work?
- Have you ever been mean to someone? Tell me about what happened.
- What is the most memorable Christmas/birthday celebration you've ever had?

TIP

Recording an interview with your grandchild is a great idea. You can be low-tech with an old tape recorder or high-tech with a computer. Try to choose a system that will last for years so you can enjoy listening to the recording for years to come.

The Examen

Ever heard of "the Examen"? No, it's not a test. It's a question originating from the *Spiritual Exercises* of St. Ignatius of Loyola. In the Examen, we look for how God is working in our lives by asking, "For what am I most grateful?" and "For what am I least grateful?" You can discuss the Examen every day at the end of the day, every month at the end of the month, or every year at the end of the year. It can help guide prayers, realize God's presence, and relinquish troubling moments that have brought confusion, guilt, or insecurity.

Sharing the Examen with your grandchild can be a wonderful opportunity for you both to share the good and the bad in your life. Here is one way to practice it.

First, find a quiet place to be together. Eliminate distractions such as the radio or TV. Then ask the question, "For what am I most grateful today?" (Or, depending on how often you see your grandchild, you could substitute "week," "month," or "year.") After you've both had a chance to think about the question, share your answers. Then ask, "For what am I least grateful today?" Take time to consider that question before answering. The answer could be as simple as "I am least grateful that my favorite shoe broke today" or as complex as "I feel my relationship with so-and-so is not as solid as I'd like it to be."

Use this conversation to guide the prayer that will follow.

When my parents passed away, my boys all either wrote or spoke at the memorial services. The theme kept resonating of the personal example their grandparents had been in their daily walk with Jesus—how they knew they were being prayed for in the good and bad times, and how much it ultimately influenced their decisions to follow God themselves. My parents weren't preachy or showy: They just walked their talk. I want to be that kind of grandparent!

—Granma Margaret P.

Spiritual Journeys

The sharing of one's spiritual journey holds many connotations. Maybe you think of testimonies around the campfire the last night of Bible camp every year. Maybe you think of *Pilgrim's Progress* or other books you've read that communicate stories about conversion and spiritual change. Have you shared your journey much with others? friends? people in your family?

Consider sharing your spiritual journey with your grandchild. You could share it in many ways. If you have numerous grandchildren spread throughout the country, type out your story and send it to everyone as a Christmas gift one year. If you have access to video or audio recording equipment (or have a child or grandchild willing to help), you could ask them to record you telling about your own journey.

Or perhaps the most intimate way is to share your story with your grandchild one-on-one. Go to a park or a quiet restaurant, or set apart some quiet time together in your home, and tell her how Jesus has influenced your life.

PROFILE

Often the most meaningful times of spiritual connection between grandparents and grandchildren don't come during planned discussions or spiritual activities but during offhand conversations and natural moments, like tucking them in at night, talking during a walk, or doing the dishes. One such experience was meaningful for Leota as she and her husband drove in the car with her granddaughter: "While riding in the car on the way to our granddaughter's confirmation," she says, "we asked her about her confirmation verse. She told us the verse she chose and why it was special to her. Then my husband shared his confirmation verse with her and I told her mine."

What an impact that small moment must have had—as Leota's granddaughter saw the words of Scripture inscribed in her grandparents' hearts many, many years after they'd chosen their own confirmation verses.

Sharing Your Journey

Don't exactly know how to start sharing your story? Maybe one of the following questions will help you start:

- When did you first learn about Jesus?

- What is your favorite Bible story—or who is your favorite Bible character? Why?

- When were you baptized? What does that mean to you now?

- What sorts of churches have you been involved in? What sorts of responsibilities have you held?

- What is the most encouraging aspect about your faith?

- What don't you understand about Christianity?

- What questions will you ask God after you die?

- When someone says "hope," what do you think of first? Why?

- What do you think about the Bible? What parts of it have been the most influential to you?

- When have you doubted Christ? What happened? How do you respond to that now?

We are trying to live out our faith in a visible way. Prayers and songs before bedtime, mealtime prayers, going to church and taking an active part in the life of the church, talking about Jesus when we take walks together, reading or telling Bible stories, and reminding our granddaughter to pray when she is not feeling well so that Jesus will make her better are all some of the visible ways we are sharing our faith.

When our grandkids are older, we hope to share more personal stories of how God has blessed us and taught us through circumstances in our lives. I (Ann) have written down my personal testimony and would like them to have that some day.

The reference to a sincere faith of a grandmother and a mother that helped shape Timothy's life in 2 Timothy 1:5 is one that I think about often as an awesome example of how important it is to be open with your faith to your children and grandchildren. I pray that we will be grandparents who really live out our faith and have teachable spirits and hearts, always remembering how important children are to our Savior.

—Grandma Ann

I have told all of my kids and grandkids about my early days—how I went to church but didn't really hear about the saving power of Jesus Christ. I have told them how one day I had a friend at work tell me about Jesus in a way I had never heard before and it changed my life. As I share this story with them, I pray that God will work in each of their lives.

—Grandpa Fred

Animal Talk

Many people like animals, and discussions about animals can be a great way for generations to connect. With your grandchild, tell stories about animals—farm animals, pets, stray dogs, that gerbil you found on your stairs one spring. If you don't have a lot of animal stories, try the following tips that can result in laughs for all ages:

- Make up names for animals (even if you don't have them) that rhyme with their type (for instance, Noodle the Poodle).

- What is the craziest name you can think of for a dog? cat? fish?

- What "rules" should people follow when naming animals? (For example: An animal should never have a name we would use for a human.)

- If you could be an animal, what would you be? Why?

- Go to a pet store or animal shelter and look at all the animals—then make up names for each one.

I think my grandmama loved my dog almost as much as I did. When we would drive down to visit, Grandmama would sit on the porch and invite Lady to come rest next to her on the bench. Even when Grandmama's eyesight was almost gone, she would tell me what a pretty dog I had.

—Matthew, grandson

Tell me a story about when you were a little girl!

Ever heard that from your grandchild? (Well, you grandpas probably haven't, but you know what we mean…)

Children want to know what life was like for you when you were their ages. What did you wear? What did you spend your time doing? What did you eat? What was church like? How were you disciplined? When were you bad? ("When were you good?" usually isn't as interesting!)

Keep a mental cabinet of your childhood stories to share with your grandchildren. When they ask for one, take it out and tell them. Then, put it away for the next grandchild.

Are you and your grandchild more gifted with images than words? Consider a shared drawing. Using the same format—the letter story—create a letter painting or drawing. You begin the picture and then send it to your grandchild for addition. Once she sends it back to you, add something else to the picture.

☞ CHECK IT OUT

Many publishers create partially written books for grandparents to fill out and give to their children or grandchildren. Here are a few for you to check out if you're interested in giving your family such a priceless gift:

- *Grandma's Memory Book* (Ancestry Publishing)

- *Grandma, Tell Me Your Memories* by Kathy Lashier

- *Grandpa, Tell Me Your Memories* by Kathy Lashier

- *Memories for My Grandchild* by Annie Decker and Nicole Stephenson

- *Grandma's Special Memories: A Keepsake Record Book* by Linda Spivey

☞ STAY CONNECTED ☞

Write fiction with your long-distance grandchild! Here's how:

Before you start, consider discussing what type of story this will be. Will it be a fairy tale? a realistic story? Do you want it to be silly? (These types of stories can easily become silly.) Do you want it to be a really great story?

Begin the story with one paragraph. Introduce the setting and maybe one character. Then send (by snail mail or e-mail) your story to your grandson. He can write the next paragraph and send it back to you for the next portion. Keep sending the story back and forth until together you fulfill the goals you set or everyone rides into the sunset living happily ever after.

Home & Garden Show

Do you watch HGTV or Food Network? Consider directing your passion for home keeping into a how-to video you make with your grandchild. Decide what you're going to do (see ideas below), and then ask an older grandchild or parent to film your episode.

Don't know where to start? Consider the following ideas:

- A multigenerational how-to cooking show. First, Grandpa can show Holly how to barbeque ribs. Then, Holly can show Grandpa how to microwave a Hot Pocket. (Insert your culinary passions in place of the ribs and Hot Pockets, of course.)

- A room renovation show. Does Grandma have a messy gardening shed? Make a film of David helping her clean her tools and organize her shed. Or shoot a video of him painting the guest bedroom (or even just cleaning out the pantry!).

- A what-not-to-wear show. Sixteen-year-old Susan can help Grandma go through her closet and then go with her to the mall for a new cool-Grandma outfit! Or Grandma can go through Susan's closet and help her select more modest outfits! (Connect this idea with 1 Timothy 2:9, which discusses modesty in dress.)

- A "reuse-this" show. If Grandpa is really gifted at finding new uses for old items, consider teaching your grandson (on film, of course) some of these new reuses.

Family Talk Show

Not a particularly handy person? You can still make a fun video with your grandchild. Consider making a family history talk show. Set up your living room furniture to look like a talk show. Then, let your grandchild be the host and interview you about your childhood. Plan funny questions together beforehand!

PROFILE

Grandma Sharon keeps a "grandmother's journal" in which she records the things her young grandsons say and do, since their mother is so busy chasing them around. One wet day, when the boys went outside, the eldest "immediately found a puddle of water, lay down in it, and started to drink the water." Even though her daughter was frustrated, Grandma Sharon "saw it from a different angle" and wrote down the funny memory. "I haven't decided when I will give her the journal," she writes, "but I think she will appreciate it whenever I do."

As much as possible, we try to take time during holidays together to share family stories. We tell our grandkids about our traditions—what life was like when we were children. We recall funny stories about their parents when they were smaller. We listen as they tell us the stories of the big things that are happening in their lives. We explain to them why we eat certain foods and remember certain people.

—Grandpa Ted

Puppet Show!

Puppets are a great way to tell stories. If your grandchild is interested in puppets, consider making some with him and then creating or writing stories together to perform with the puppets.

Look for simple ideas on the Internet for homemade puppets created with simple, practical supplies such as film canisters or prescription bottles, juice cans, paper plates, and (of course) socks. You can create a family of similar puppets or a huge variety of types, shapes, and colors.

Make a puppet stage out of a large cardboard box. Paint it, cut out a hole for the stage, and put some fabric over the hole for the curtain.

Create a story with your grandchild (see "Great Puppet Show Ideas" on this page) that the two of you can perform for other friends or family members. Remember to have fun developing interesting puppet characters and personalities!

Great Puppet Show Ideas

- retelling of a fairy tale
- adaptation of a family story, such as how Grandma and Grandpa met
- adaptation of a Bible story
- appropriate holiday story, such as the Nativity or the Boston Tea Party
- fictional account of Grandma and Marcy's trip to the moon!
- a puppet song-and-dance show

The hurdle is that none of our grandchildren have grown up close to us. The nearest are three hours away and four are in Texas.

I cut out an activity section from our Sunday comics, and once in a while I send it to the kids. It only costs the price of a stamp, and kids love to receive mail! If you have some extra coupons that you know the mom can use, you can add them to the envelope to show you're thinking about everyone!

—Grandma Jane, grandmother of 11

When I was working overseas, I accidentally fell in with a friendly cult. My grandmother heard about this and her concern for my soul prompted her to send me several care packages filled with washcloths, Mrs. Grass soup mix, and cult-opposing literature. I was deeply blessed by her very practical concern for my whole being.

—Matthew, grandson

One time, Grandfather took my hand and we walked to the corner grocery story. He gave me a penny to put into the gum machine.

—Grandma Eileen, grandmother of 16, great-grandmother of five

🔘 **STAY CONNECTED** 🔘

An Ongoing Story

Snail mail may be out of fashion these days, but writing letters to your grandchildren—especially if you live far away from them—can be one of the most meaningful ways you can connect with them over the years. Both preschoolers and teenagers will smile and feel special when something arrives in the mail addressed just to them! And as you write regularly, a "story" unfolds between the two of you: a record of the happenings in your life, your thoughts on recent events, your questions and concerns, your hopes and dreams, your words of love and encouragement.

If you have multiple grandchildren, consider committing to write each of them a letter or card once a month; make it easy by pre-addressing the envelopes and paper-clipping them to your calendar to remind you.

Set aside a shoe box in which you can keep—and treasure—any correspondence you receive from your grandchildren. These letters will be meaningful keepsakes for them to read when they are grown-up. Also, ask your children to keep the letters you send to your grandkids; perhaps the grandkids can each have their own shoe box in their closet for letters from you. Decades into the future, these messages of love will speak into their lives.

Add pizazz to the letters and cards you send in the mail. Here are 12 fun ideas—you could try one each month!

- Make your own envelope out of a magazine page, old calendar, or sturdy wrapping paper.

- Write your letter in a secret code, and include the cipher at the bottom. (Merely create simple drawings that correspond with each letter in the alphabet.)

- Include confetti in the letter so that it falls out when your grandchild opens it.

- Include a children's poem, limerick, riddle, or joke with your letter.

- Send a postcard you've created by cutting apart a cereal box. (Check at the post office to make sure you've affixed the correct postage.)

- In the spring, send a packet of seeds for your grandchild to plant.

- Buy and send a simple bookmark for your grandchild with your letter.

- Send a musical card—one that plays a song when it's opened—to delight your grandchild!

- Include favorite stickers and recent photos with a letter.

- Photocopy your hand, and then write your note on the other side of the paper. Tell your grandchild you are sending a "high five"!

- Instead of sending words, create and send a collage of images from magazines that your grandchild might like.

TIP

You can make letter writing easier for your grandchild by giving him 12 pre-addressed and stamped envelopes with cards that he can use to write back to you. This will communicate to your grandchild how important and special it is for you to receive letters and notes from him.

I remember my Grandmama regularly writing me letters as a child. When I was in grade school, I would read her teacherlike printing. As I grew up, I graduated to her cursive. Her letters told of the daily activities of her life. At the end she always reminded me that she and Papa loved me.

—Liebe, granddaughter

My maternal grandma was an incredible little woman. She wrote me regularly when I was away at school, and she always scotch-taped a dime to the letter—letters that never had any punctuation but were packed with love.

—Grandpa Charles, grandfather of 17

Speak Into the Future

Write your grandchildren letters that they won't see until they're grown. As each grandchild's birthday nears, take time to reflect on how special that grandchild is to you and how much you love him. Write a one-page letter to your grandchild describing what he is like at the current age, naming your hopes and dreams for him, communicating your constant love, and speaking of your faith. Your intention, though, will be to save the letter for a future date. You may plan to give all the letters to your grandchild when he graduates from high school or when he turns 21. Or you may choose to save these letters with your will, indicating that they are to be given to each grandchild upon your death. This is a powerful way to continue to speak in their lives even after you're gone.

I remember that when we first saw our granddaughter Sadie, we thought of Scripture—how she was beautifully and wonderfully made and how God knew every hair on her head before she was born. It was a beautiful reminder that each person has purpose in God's eyes.

—Boyd and Karen, new grandparents

Read, Watch, Listen, Tell

Connecting Through Books and Movies

Sometimes connecting with grandkids is easy and happens naturally. But other times it's not quite so easy. Ever had a conversation like this?

Grandparent: How are you doing?
Grandchild: Fine.
Grandparent: How's school?
Grandchild: Fine.
Grandparent: How's soccer going?
Grandchild: OK.
Grandparent: Anything else going on?
Grandchild: Not really.
Grandparent: Well, I'm glad you're doing well. I love you.
Grandchild: You, too.
Grandparent: Talk to you soon.
Grandchild: 'Bye.

Sometimes the generation gap looms so large it seems impassable. But books and movies can serve as a powerful bridge between the two of you. As you read books or watch movies together, you're sharing an experience that's always sure to be full of connection points. You can talk about your favorite scenes or characters; you can laugh about hysterical moments; you can munch on popcorn as you build a memory.

The stories that speak to you—and to them—will help you speak to each other.

Books

The Main Character: You!

With a digital camera and some computer skills, you can create a book with your grandchild that your whole family will love. First, work together with your grandchild to write a simple fictional story (such as a modern fairy tale) or a nonfiction retelling of an experience you and your grandchild shared. Be sure to include other family members (and pets) along with locations nearby in your story, such as a favorite ice cream shop, a park, or your backyard. Then take photos together that will accompany the story—or select digital photos you've already got.

Next, go online to select a website for making photo books that's right for you. The companies that sponsor these sites make it easy to design your book, input the story, and add the pictures. Once you're done, you order as many copies as you want and the company sends them to you as high-quality, nicely bound books.

Of course, you can always make your own book with a binder, nice paper, and handwritten text. The level of complexity is up to you!

☞ CHECK IT OUT

Here are two sites we recommend:
- www.shutterfly.com
- www.lulu.com

STAY CONNECTED

Nothing beats sitting on Grandpa or Grandma's lap to hear a story! But if you're far away and not able to see your grandchildren often, here's an idea that's a close second. Buy your grandchild a subscription to a fun magazine—he will be excited to receive it in the mail each month. Be sure to ask your grandchild what he read (or looked at) in the magazine, and ask your grandchild to tell you what he has learned from it. This is a fun way to share the experience of reading, even across the miles.

CHECK IT OUT

There are lots of great kids magazines available; here are a few of our favorites:

For Infants to Age 4

- **Wild Animal Baby**—Designed to introduce babies to images and concepts from nature, this magazine looks much more like a board book. Its pages are easy for small hands to turn, and the pictures are colorful and bright.

- **Babybug**—Created for little ones, this magazine contains fun read-alouds, rhymes, finger plays, and other stories to introduce young children to the fun of reading, listening, and learning.

For Preschoolers and Kindergarteners

- **Your Big Backyard**—Full of stunning animal photography, this magazine nurtures an appreciation of nature; it also includes ideas for crafts and family activities.

- **Click**—This science magazine for kids draws out their natural curiosity about the world and introduces them to science concepts in exciting, surprising ways.

- **Ladybug**—Meant to build a love of reading, Ladybug is full of short stories, poems, and pictures by award-winning authors and illustrators.

- **Highlights High Five**—This preschool version of the much-loved Highlights magazine contains read-aloud stories, activities, and puzzles to help young kids get started on the path to learning.

For Early Elementary–Age Kids

- **National Geographic Kids**—A creative kids' version of the grown-up magazine, NG Kids introduces children to geography, world cultures, and lots of plants and animals. Each issue comes with animal collector cards.

- **Ranger Rick**—The next step "up" from Your Big Backyard, Ranger Rick contains amazing images of animals as well as fun stories and information about nature.

- **Clubhouse Jr.**—This Christian magazine includes stories, craft ideas, puzzles, and fun activities for young children that are meant to reinforce biblical values.

- **Ask**—This exciting magazine is full of interesting information about science, history, and more. Built on children's natural curiosity, this magazine helps children learn more about the world in engaging, adventurous ways.

- **Highlights**—Full of stories, puzzles, jokes, crafts, science experiments, and more, this magazine provides hours of reading and fun.

Upper Elementary–Age Kids

- **Cricket**—This classic magazine provides hours of reading fun for kids, including poems, folk tales, adventure stories, biographical sketches, and fun fiction.

- **Highlights**—Full of stories, puzzles, jokes, crafts, science experiments, and more, this magazine provides hours of reading and fun.

- **Clubhouse**—This Christian magazine has engaging articles, puzzles, and family activities. Clubhouse focuses on instilling Christian values in young people.

I am amazed at what a great job my kids and kids-in-law are doing. It brings a deep sense of gratitude that God did answer my desperate (at times) prayers for wisdom when I see the men of God they have become and the women they chose as life partners.

—Granma Margaret P.

Personal Library

If you're a book lover, consider creating a library for each of your grandchildren by buying them a nice, hardcover edition of a literary classic each year at Christmas time. These books can be saved for future use; when your grandchildren become adults, they'll have a great collection of valuable books to read and treasure!

The Best Thing About Being a Grandparent

- The best thing is being able to be an encourager, supporter, and—from time to time—a partner on their journey.—Grandpa Walt

- We get to be an unconditionally loving and "safe" place for the kids—it's a way we can model what Jesus is like. We also receive unconditional love from the kids!—Pops Bob and Grams Jeanne

- One of the most rewarding things is that when I visit my grandkids they will run and yell, "Grandpa! Grandpa!" What is better than that?—Grandpa Fred

- I love their unconditional love for me; they watch and listen to what I do, and as preschoolers they love to copy me, listen to me, and be with me.—Grams Kay

- We don't have to worry about whether the grandchildren have clean underwear on (in case they get taken to a hospital and embarrass us) or whether they did their chores or what they are supposed to do tomorrow. We don't have to make sure they eat all the right things. We just have to love them and encourage them. We get to share what comes closest to God's love for us—we can love them without condition.—Grandpa Ted

- Grandchildren are one of the most precious gifts God had given us, outside of our own children! Having been through the child-rearing process, it's enjoyable to watch our grandchildren grow and learn from a different perspective, one with less pressure and more time to laugh and love and be silly. It's like watching plants in a garden with all the different stages of growth—life has come full circle!—Grandpa Jim and Grandma Ann

Teddy Bear Picnic

Invite your grandchild to bring over a teddy bear (or two or three) for a special story time with you. Plan a simple "teddy bear picnic" that you can eat outdoors; include some of your grandchild's favorite foods. As you eat together, pretend the teddy bear is also a guest and have imaginary conversations with it. Then read a teddy bear storybook together, such as *The Teddy Bears' Picnic* by Jimmy Kennedy, illustrated by Alexandra Day, or *Corduroy* by Don Freeman.

If there's a special book that a grandchild loves, I enjoy recording a tape of myself reading it so my grandchild can listen to it at home.

I remember discovering how closely my grandson Zachary listened to the tape of his favorite book I'd recorded. Once, when I was reading it to him in person, I paraphrased part of the story. Zachary corrected me immediately the first time I altered a sentence! I read aloud word for word after that because I realized Zachary had memorized the tape.

—Grandma Carolyn

Homework Help

Get a copy of your grandchildren's reading list from school, and then plan to read one of the books they'll be discussing in class. You can talk about the characters and plot together, and maybe even "help" with homework!

Back in the Good Ol' Days...

What were your favorite books as a young child? Many of the classic novels that you may have read are still in print and are enduring favorites. Introduce your grandchildren to easy, classic chapter books such as the following:

- *The Boxcar Children* series by Gertrude Chandler Warner
- *The Little House on the Prairie* series by Laura Ingalls Wilder
- The *Trixie Belden* series by Julie Campbell
- *The Hardy Boys* series by Franklin W. Dixon
- The *Nancy Drew* series by Carolyn Keene

PROFILE

My granddaughter Jamie and I wrote a book together. When she was still in grade school, she loved to make up stories. I had a chance to spend time with her, helping her shape and write her stories. We talked about the structure of a story, how characters progress, and how the story moves along. We thought through what it means to have a conflict or quest in a story to keep it interesting.

As Jamie told me her story, I would type it, making minor adjustments as we went along. When the story was finished, we looked for graphics that would illustrate the story. One of her stories was about an elephant that found an abandoned ostrich egg and tried to hatch it. Of course, it broke; all the animals tried to blame someone, and so on. So we found illustrations of an egg and an elephant. Then we set it all up in a word processing program and printed the story with the illustrations.

I wrote some of my own stories, too. We collected the stories into a book, made some copies, bound them with a spiral binder, made an illustrated cover for the book, and shared it with the family.

The book and the memories of the project remain dear to me—and Jamie *still* tells and writes good stories!

—Grandpa Ted

Help Grandchildren Understand Aging, Illness, or Loss

Sometimes reading stories together can be the best way to open up doors of conversation or help children deal with their feelings about difficult issues like a grandparent becoming ill or coping with a beloved grandparent's death. These books can serve as powerful avenues of understanding and healing for grandchildren:

* Johnston, Tony. *Yonder.* In this story, a family plants trees to mark both happy and sad milestones—births, marriages, and deaths. Upon his death, the grandfather is buried under a tree he had planted as young man—which highlights the bond between generations.

* Kadono, Eiko. *Grandpa's Soup.* Grandfather is discouraged and lonely after Grandmother's death, but he eventually decides to try his hand at making her famous soup. His first try is a failure, but in each attempt he improves—and remembers a bit of her recipe. And as he cooks and eats, his loneliness is assuaged as he shares his food with animals and neighbors.

* Shriver, Maria. *What's Happening to Grandpa?* When Grandpa begins to suffer from Alzheimer's, young granddaughter Kate decides to help him by making a scrapbook with him of his photos and memories of his life.

* Wangerin, Walter, Jr. *I Am My Grandpa's Enkelin.* A granddaughter recalls all the things her German American grandfather taught her. Most important, he showed her that his death was not an ending, but a beginning.

Draw Out the Artist Within

If your grandchildren are interested in art, or even if they simply enjoy coloring, visit your local library and check out several Caldecott Medal or Caldecott Honor winners. The Caldecott Medal is awarded annually by the American Library Association to one children's book with outstanding illustrations. Most libraries have a list of Caldecott award winners.

Enjoy reading several of the books together and comparing the illustrations. Then, if you'd like, try to copy one of the illustrations together with paper and crayons—or simply mimic one illustrator's style as you each draw your own picture together.

If we have to travel long distances with our grandchildren, we listen to audio books. Junie B. Jones has been fun or the Focus on the Family Adventures in Odyssey series is good. We're not into having a TV in the car.

—Grandma Jane

Pray & Play Bible and *Pray & Play Bible 2* (Group Publishing) are awesome resources that can help you connect with preschool-age grandchildren and introduce them to your faith in Jesus. The *Pray & Play Bible* books have large, colorful illustrations and short picture book–like retellings of important New Testament and Old Testament stories. But the features that really make these books stand out are the activity and experience suggestions that follow each story. You'll find easy-to-sing Bible-story songs, crafts, recipes, prayers, service ideas, worship ideas, and much more! All of the ideas are appropriate for little kids. Together you can put your faith into action!

Explore the Big Issues

Some of the greatest books for preteens and young teenagers are the Newbery Medal and Newbery Honor books. These books are selected annually by the American Library Association and are well-written novels for older children that draw on themes that reflect some of the big issues of life, such as

- love and friendship
- dealing with the death of a loved one
- injustice (such as racism or persecution)
- poverty and wealth
- family relationships
- self-esteem
- God's existence

Some of these books are controversial and many of them reflect a non-Christian worldview; however, even those that are most controversial can lead into powerful avenues of discussion. Consider reading a Newbery award winner in tandem with your grandchild, and take time to discuss the issues together. Invite your grandchild to share his reactions, thoughts, or questions from what he has read; share from your own experiences about some of these themes and tough issues.

Some Newbery award winners are written by Christian authors, and others have themes that will naturally lend themselves to powerful spiritual conversations. Here are a few that we recommend for discussion with older kids:

- *Crispin: The Cross of Lead* by Avi
- *Holes* by Louis Sachar
- *Jacob Have I Loved* and *Bridge to Terabithia* by Katherine Paterson
- *A Single Shard* by Linda Sue Park
- *A Wrinkle in Time* by Madeleine L'Engle

PASS IT ON

As you create art together or discuss what you observe about the work of the artists who illustrated the Caldecott-award-winning books, you may want to share with your grandchild what it means to you that God is an artist. Help your grandchild realize how special she is by saying something like, "God is the great artist who created everything in the world. Did you know that you are God's work of art? You are God's masterpiece."

You may want to share Isaiah 64:8 with your grandchild; it reads, "And yet, O Lord, you are our Father. We are the clay, and you are the potter. We all are formed by your hand."

You could delve deeper into this line of conversation by asking open-ended questions such as

• What are some things you see in nature that show you that God is an artist? Why do they stand out to you?

• How does it feel to know that you are God's artistic masterpiece?

 BRIDGE BUILDER

Here are some great questions to ask your grandchild when you're reading a novel together:

• On a scale of 1 to 10, how would you rate this book? Why?

• Which character do you relate to the most? Why?

• Which character do you think is most like me? Why?

• What's your favorite part in the story? Why do you like it so much?

• Were there any parts you didn't like? What didn't you like about them?

• What do you think is the main point of the book?

• Were there any scenes that scared you or bothered you? What were they?

• What does this book say about our world? Do you agree with its message? Why or why not?

PROFILE

Gramps Steve says, "I love to put my grandchildren to bed and tell them bedtime stories." Using funny voices, animated gestures, and discussion questions, Gramps enlivens and exaggerates classic stories like "The Three Little Pigs" and "Goldilocks and the Three Bears."

"Their mother tells me I rev them up too much with my stories. But I think I'm just tiring them out so they sleep better," says Steve. "I end each night with prayer, a hug and a kiss, and an 'I love you.'" It doesn't get much better than that.

By 3 years old, Jacob had already developed a rather phenomenal stubborn streak that often tended to obscure his cuddly heart. At our first ever Pinney family reunion, I had at one point collapsed in exhaustion on the large sofa in our rented cabin. Suddenly, I felt little hands on my arms. "Are you tired, Granma? Here, let me tuck you in. You can use my blanket." This blanket was a deep source of security for this rascal, so the sacrifice was significant. Then he proceeded to curl up beside me!

—Granma Margaret P.

On-the-Spot Authors!

David Wiesner is an award-winning illustrator who creates amazing wordless books. These books use fabulous pictures to tell a story—and they also leave a lot up to the reader's imagination! Get some of these great David Wiesner books and "read" them with your grandchildren by together making up the narrative that goes with each page. The story could be different every time you "read" it!

Visit Grandma...With a Favorite Character!

Some of the best-loved characters in illustrated children's books make visits to their grandparents' house. If your young grandchild loves one of these characters, read one of these books together the next time she comes to visit:

- Little Bear: *To Grandmother's House* by Maurice Sendak
- Little Critter: *Grandma, Grandpa, and Me; Just Fishing With Grandma; Just Grandma and Me* by Mercer Mayer
- Spot: *Spot Visits His Grandparents; Spot and His Grandma; Spot Loves His Grandma; Spot Loves His Grandpa* by Eric Hill
- Arthur: *Arthur's Chicken Pox* by Marc Brown

PROFILE

As a busy mom, Karen treasured her own mother's role as grandma in her children's lives. She recalls, "My mom prayed for each of her children and grandchildren by name every day. She may not have known what was going on in each of their lives, but she knew that God knew. That prayer life gave her a purpose in her later years of life, especially when she reached the point that she could no longer walk.

"I remember at one point she was very near death; I told her she needed to pray for her granddaughter Jennifer, as she was going through the medical school application and interview process. That reminded her that she still had a significant purpose in life, and she went on to live two more years."

12 Top-Notch Grandparent-Themed Books

These fun books for kids portray silly adventures, meaningful memories, and great loving relationships between grandparents and grandchildren. Bring this list along the next time you visit the library, and check out a few to read with your grandkids!

1. Canyon, Christopher. *Grandma's Feather Bed.* Children love looking at the detailed illustrations in this book (based on the John Denver song of the same name) and also learning about old ways—like feather beds, ticking, and homemade butter.

2. Carney, Margaret. *At Grandpa's Sugar Bush.* A young boy makes maple syrup with his grandfather in the old-fashioned way.

3. Crystal, Billy. *I Already Know I Love You.* Written for his soon-to-be-born grandchild, this book expresses the excitement and hope of expectant grandparents and the enduring love they have for each and every grandchild.

4. Dunbar, James and Martin Remphry. *When I Was Young.* Josh asks his grandma about what life was like when she was young; Grandma's stories reach back through the generations, and Josh learns amazing family stories stretching back to the 1600s.

5. Greenfield, Eloise. *Grandpa's Face.* Tamika loves her actor grandfather's expressive face. But when she spies him making a hardened, angry expression as he practices for a scene, she is bewildered to see such cruel emotions on his face! In this story, she discovers the difference between acting and her grandfather's real-life love for her.

6. Gritz, Ona. *Tangerines and Tea, My Grandparents and Me.* This fun and creative book uses imaginative alliteration and the alphabet to recall fun experiences grandchildren have with their grandparents.

7. Juster, Norton. *The Hello, Goodbye Window.* The window at Grandma and Grandpa's house is a very special place—you can look at the stars, you can spot the pizza delivery guy, but most important, you can wave hello and goodbye. This Caldecott Medal winner highlights the magic of "everyday" moments shared between grandparents and grandchildren.

8. McCaughrean, Geraldine. *My Grandmother's Clock.* In this playful tale, a grandmother tells how she keeps track of time—even though her clock is broken!

9. Oberman, Sheldon. *The Always Prayer Shawl.* In this story, a Jewish prayer shawl is passed from generation to generation—and along with the shawl come memories, tradition, and faith. While the family moves from czarist Russia to America, young Adam learns that though circumstances may change, some things—love, faith, and tradition—*never* change.

10. Rabun, Miles and William. *My Grandma's Backyard.* When Miles and William visit their grandma's house, they have lots of fun in her backyard. This is a particularly inspiring book because the authors, children, are writing about their own experience.

11. Schwartz, David M. *Super Grandpa.* When 66-year-old Gustaf Hakansson is rejected by the Tour of Sweden in 1951, he proved that he could do it by cycling to the start of the race (600 miles!) and then winning the 1,000-mile race itself. This amazing tale is based on a true—and inspiring—story.

12. Spinelli, Eileen. *Something to Tell the Grandcows.* Emmadine (a cow) wishes she had exciting stories to tell her grandcows, so she decides to go on an expedition to the South Pole!

We do not see ourselves as correctors, though we insist that our standards be met when our grandchildren are in our house.

—Grandpa Charles, grandfather of 17

Movies

 BRIDGE BUILDER

Back in the Day...

Show your grandchildren old home movies of when your kids were young—or, if you have old slides, do a slideshow! Your grandkids have probably never seen slides projected onto a screen (or wall)—they'll love it! Use the experience to tell silly stories about your childhood, your kids' childhood, and the similarities to or differences from your grandchildren's experiences.

One for the Road

Locate an old-fashioned drive-in theater and plan to take your grandchildren to a movie there during an upcoming visit. Make sure the movie is appropriate for kids, and then load 'em up in the car, bring some snacks and blankets along, and go to the show. As you drive, talk about your own memories of attending a drive-in theater as a child or teenager.

What's Your Favorite?

Get to know your grandchild better by inviting him to select one of his favorite movies from the video store, and then watch it together. As you watch the movie, use the opportunity to get to know more about who your grandchild is and what his interests are. What themes in the movie do you think attract your grandchild most? Which characters, events, or themes seem to connect most with your grandchild?

Even if you don't like the movie much, keep those thoughts to yourself and focus on drawing out the best elements of the film. Recount favorite scenes together and ask simple questions (before or after the movie) about why your grandchild enjoys the movie so much.

Movie Discussion Ideas

Movies can really speak to the heart. As you watch a great story unfold on the screen with your grandchild, you can share a special experience of laughing together, rooting for the hero, and, of course, munching on some popcorn. Watching movies together can also open up great doors of conversation—you can talk about important issues as you explore favorite characters, plot twists, and the movie's themes and lessons. Here are just a few suggestions of movies you can watch and talk about with your grandchildren.

God's Great World

The BBC and the Discovery Channel teamed together to create an amazing series called *Planet Earth* that contains groundbreaking footage of nature. The images are compelling, the quality is stunning, and both kids and grown-ups will be amazed as they get a tour of places on the Earth that are untouched by humans.

Some of the episodes contain short segments of predators hunting prey, so you may need to fast-forward if you're watching the movie with young children. Also, occasionally the narrator talks about the theory of evolution, so you may want to be prepared to briefly clarify with your grandchildren your own beliefs about the creation/evolution debate. All things considered, though, these movies are well worth watching. The dazzling beauty of God's creation revealed in *Planet Earth*'s footage will leave a strong impression on your grandchildren—and you, too!

As you watch the movie together, you may want to point out how the beauty of God's creation prompts you to want to worship him. You could also share Romans 1:20, explaining that we can see proof of God's existence and power in the awesome world he created.

☞ CHECK IT OUT

For movie nights that include kid-friendly recipes that follow the theme of the movie, along with discussion questions, decorating ideas, Scripture passages, trivia quizzes, and more, grab a copy of *Group's Dinner and a Movie: G-Rated* (Group Publishing). The book includes ideas for 12 different movie nights you and your grandkids of all ages will enjoy!

Pre-K and Early Elementary–Age Grandchildren

Horton Hears a Who!

Rating: G

Plot: Horton, a friendly elephant, discovers that a tiny community of creatures—the Whos—live on a minuscule speck of dust. Horton takes it upon himself to protect the speck of dust and take it to Mount Nool where it will be safe. Along the way, Horton deals with Kangaroo, who refuses to believe in the Whos' existence.

TIP

Each of these suggestions of movies to watch includes possible discussion questions as conversation starters. But remember, it's always best to let the conversation take its natural course—start with a question, and then see where things go on their own as you and your grandchild enjoy the experience of watching a movie together.

Discussion Theme: Believing without seeing

Discussion Points:

- The Whos have a hard time "believing" in Horton (who they cannot see); Kangaroo refuses to believe in the Whos (who she cannot see). Talk with your grandchild about what it means to believe in things we cannot see. Share about your own belief in God, even though you cannot literally see him.

- You may want to share John 20:29 as you encourage your grandchild to believe in God even though she cannot see him.

- Ask: What are some things in our world that show you God exists even though we can't see him?

One of my favorite times with my grandson was taking him to see *Horton Hears a Who!* This was one of my favorite books as a boy. I loved telling him the story before the movie, holding him on my lap when he was scared, and laughing together at the funny parts. I especially loved talking afterward about the story and how everyone is important no matter how small, and then telling him how important he is to me and to God.

—Pops Bob

The Pirates Who Don't Do Anything

Rating: G

Plot: This *Veggie Tales* movie tells the story of three pirates—Elliot, Sedgewick, and George—who are hopelessly unequipped for the task ahead of them: a heroic trek to save a kidnapped boy. But eventually, with the King's help, they rise to the challenge before them—and provide lots of laughs along the way.

Discussion Theme: God using flawed people to do great things

Discussion Points:

- Sedgewick, Elliot, and George all have flaws and failings: One is easily frightened, one has chronic low self-esteem, and one is lazy. Discuss their "problems" with your grandchild, and then use the opportunity to communicate the truth that no one is perfect—but God can still use imperfect people!

- Ask: What were some of the challenges the (good) pirates faced? (Point out how the challenges strengthened them.)

- In the movie, the king says, "The hero is the one who does what's right—no matter how hard it is." Talk with your grandchild about times it may be hard to do what's right, trying to focus on situations he might experience at his young age.

- Discuss how the heroes of the Bible were just regular people who trusted in God. Talk about your favorite Bible heroes together, and emphasize that God used them and empowered them to accomplish great things. (You may want to use Hebrews 11 as a list of Bible heroes you could talk about.)

- Ask: How do you think God may want to use *you* to do great things for him?

Nim's Island

Rating: PG

Plot: Nim is a young girl who lives on an island with her marine biologist father and dreams of adventure. She develops a friendship via e-mail with Alex (Alexandra) Rover, the author of her favorite adventure books. When a monsoon strikes the island, Alexandra arrives to "help"—though ironically, this adventure-books author has extreme phobias about nearly everything! In her efforts to help Nim, Alexandra faces and overcomes her own fears.

Discussion Theme: Facing fears with courage

Discussion Points:

- Nim loves to read adventure books. Discuss favorite books with your grandchild: Who are her favorite characters? What adventures (from favorite books) would she most like to have?

- Alexandra Rover has an overabundance of fears. Ask your grandchild: What are you afraid of? Empathize with your grandchild and, if appropriate, share some fears you had as a young child.

- In the movie, Nim's dad talks about how courage has to do with choices we make on a daily basis. Talk about courageous choices together, such as deciding to be kind to a bully or choosing to trust God at night if a child is afraid of the dark.

- Sometimes young children misunderstand courage, thinking it means not being afraid in a scary situation. In reality, courageous people *do* experience fear—they just don't let it stop them from doing what is right. Discuss what courage means to you; share a time when you did something courageous.

- You may want to share 2 Timothy 1:7 and talk about how true courage comes from God.

How to Eat Fried Worms

Rating: PG

Plot: Billy Forrester has moved to a new school and rather quickly finds himself the target of bullies who've filled his thermos with worms. In an attempt to keep his pride, Billy claims he doesn't mind worms—in fact, he loves to eat them! This sets the stage for a worm-eating contest and a lot of gross-out humor. In the end, many of the former bullies become friends with Billy as they admire his determination to be true to himself.

Discussion Theme: Fitting in...or *not* fitting in

Discussion Points:

- As the new kid in school, Billy didn't "fit in." Tell your grandchild about times in your life when you felt like you didn't fit in. Invite your grandchild to share about times he didn't fit in. Reassure your grandchild that you know it can be emotionally painful to feel like an outsider.

- Why do you think Joe was such a bully? Are there kids at your school who are bullies? Why do you think they are like that?

- Do you think Billy did the right thing when he told the bullies he liked to eat worms? Why or why not?

- Why do you think Joe's friends started to become Billy's friends?

- If you think your grandchild may be experiencing bullying, talk with him about the best ways to handle it, such as standing up to the bully (as in the movie) or going to adult authorities (like parents or teachers).

- You may want to add to the laughs by telling your grandchild that some people in the Bible ate really gross stuff, too, especially John the Baptist (see Matthew 3:4)!

Boys' Night!
How to Eat Fried Worms is the kind of movie young boys love—lots of laughs, lots of things to gag about, and lots of fun! Make it a special "boys' night" by eating worms for dinner (spaghetti) and then worms-in-dirt for dessert (gummy worms in chocolate pudding with crushed Oreo cookies mixed in).

The Lion, the Witch, and the Wardrobe

Rating: PG

Plot: Based on C.S. Lewis' classic, this movie tells the story of Lucy, Edmund, Susan, and Peter and their adventures in the magical land of Narnia. Edmund betrays his siblings to the White Witch; Aslan (the Christ figure in the story) sacrifices himself rather than let Edmund be executed for his treachery. Eager to redeem himself, Edmund fights valiantly in battle. Shadowing the biblical resurrection story, Aslan returns to life and leads the Narnians in defeating the White Witch's army.

Discussion Theme: Guilt and forgiveness

Discussion Points:

- This movie does a good job of portraying the bitterness and frustration that led Edmund to betray his siblings. Invite your grandchild to consider whether she can relate to Edmund. Has she ever let jealousy, anger, or selfishness get the best of her?

- Share from your own experience about a time you did something you regretted; talk frankly about the feelings of guilt and shame that accompanied that action.

- What was Aslan like? What did you like about him?

- Do you think it was hard for Peter, Susan, and Lucy to forgive Edmund? Do you think it was hard for Edmund to forgive himself? Why?

- Point out the correlation between Aslan's death and resurrection and Christ's. Invite your grandchild to share what connections between the story and the account of Christ stand out to her.

- You may want to share John 3:16 and talk with your grandchild about what Christ's forgiveness means to you and how it has affected your life.

During the winter Olympics, I watched downhill skiing with my husband and his grandma. Every time one of the athletes prepared to ski down the slopes, Grandma would tense up and say, "Oh, I just don't think I could do that. I'm sure my knees just couldn't take it." I imagined the commentator saying, "And next up is . . . Grandma!" And Grandma would be bravely standing at the top of the hill hoping her knees would not give out.

—Liebe, granddaughter-in-law

Teenage Grandchildren

August Rush

Rating: PG

Plot: Evan Taylor is an orphan who is certain his parents are alive and are coming to find him. In an effort to find them himself, Evan ends up lost in New York City, where he discovers music. Evan is an instant prodigy, and music becomes his deepest passion, rivaled only by his drive to reunite with his parents. Through several twists and turns, Evan's parents find him—and each other—in a touching finale.

Discussion Theme: God-given abilities, talents, and passions

Discussion Points:

- Though contrived at times, this movie inspires its viewers to connect with their own talents just as Evan discovered his passion for music. Invite your grandchild to talk about his talents, passions, and abilities. Use the opportunity to encourage and affirm him.

- What do you think was more important to Evan—playing music or finding his parents? Why?

- What are your biggest dreams in life?

- Share what your talents, hobbies, or interests were when you were a teenager; reflect on how they compare or contrast with your talents and interests today.

- You may want to share ideas from 1 Corinthians 12 as you talk about how God gives each Christian spiritual gifts along with natural gifts, talents, and abilities.

Becoming Jane

Rating: PG

Plot: This retelling of the life of the famous novelist (and spinster) Jane Austen mixes historical biography with themes and characters from her novels—and adds a good deal of fiction along the way—to create the love story that may have been. At a time in history when a good match was economically necessary for upper-middle-class families like Jane's, she falls for Tom, who is not quite wealthy enough. (He is financially dependent on his wealthy uncle.) Jane and Tom fall in love in a context much like Austen's novels—in which propriety, manners, and restraint rule the day.

Discussion Theme: True love

Discussion Points:

- Marrying for love was considered a silly idea in Jane Austen's time, but she believed in it. Ask: Do you think love is the most important reason to marry someone? Why or why not? What are some other important reasons?

- Tell your grandchild about when you and your spouse met and fell in love. Share how it was like or unlike the love story in the movie.

- Talk with your grandchild about her "dream" spouse—what kind of person does she want to marry? Why?

- Celebrate romantic love together by keeping God a part of the conversation. Help your grandchild feel comfortable with her romantic feelings by affirming that God created romantic love.

- You may want to talk about 1 Corinthians 13:4-7 and discuss how it relates to various "kinds" of love: God's love for us, our love for each other, and romantic love.

Girls' Night!

Becoming Jane is a great love story for a movie night between a grandmother and her teenage granddaughter. Consider starting with a formal English tea (scones, clotted cream, and tea); then fix each other's hair and makeup for a formal picture together a la Jane Austen.

We Are Marshall

Rating: PG

Plot: Based on a true story, this movie recounts the events that followed a tragic plane crash in 1970 that killed the entire football team of Marshall University. After the accident, the town and school are understandably devastated. But when the school administration determines it's best to cut the football program entirely, a student becomes equally determined to rebuild the team. A new coach is hired and the program is relaunched from the ground up. Despite the many challenges in their way, the new players learn to work together and discover the value of striving to overcome adversity.

Discussion Theme: Perseverance and determination

Discussion Points:

- Which character did you most relate to? Why?

- Do you think you'd want to play on the new Marshall team? Why or why not?

- What's the toughest challenge you've faced so far in your life? How did you get through it (or how are you trying to get through it)?

- Tell your grandchild about a time you persevered through a trial, disappointment, or heartbreak.

- You may want to share Romans 5:1-5 and talk with your grandchild about spiritual perseverance and the powerful effect challenges can have on our faith.

- Who most inspires you from this story? Why?

For more amazing resources

visit us at
group.com...

...or call us at
1-800-447-1070

Group
Incredible things will happen®